# Start Your Side Hustle Today

I0408539

*Thea Stewart*

Member of PageTitans

**Please don't forget to follow me on Amazon:**

https://amazon.com/author/theiastewart

We would greatly appreciate it if you could provide a review as we love to receive feedback from our customers. Thank you.

# Table of Contents

| Side Hustle | Knowledge Needed | Money Needed | Profit Potential |
|---|---|---|---|
| Dog walking and pet sitting service | Low | Low | Low |
| House cleaning and organization service | Low | Low | Low |
| Lawn mowing and gardening service | Low | Low | Low |
| Car washing and detailing service | Low | Low | Low |
| Renting out a room or property on Airbnb | Low | Low | Low |
| Running errands for busy individuals | Low | Low | Low |
| Selling handmade crafts on Etsy | Low | Low | Low |
| Reselling thrift store finds online | Low | Low | Low |
| Participating in online surveys or market research | Low | Low | Low |
| Renting out your car or unused parking space | Low | Low | Low |
| Data entry and virtual assisting services | Low | Low | Low |
| House or pet sitting for neighbors or friends | Low | Low | Low |
| Starting a neighborhood cleaning service | Low | Low | Low |
| Running a lemonade stand or selling baked goods | Low | Low | Low |
| Offering carpool services for busy parents or coworkers | Low | Low | Low |
| Renting out camping equipment or outdoor gear | Low | Low | Low |
| Organizing garage sales for others | Low | Low | Low |
| Providing basic landscaping services | Low | Low | Low |
| Creating and selling digital art or designs | Low | Low | Low |
| Providing graphic design services | Low | Low | Low |
| Freelance writing or content creation | Medium | Low | Low |
| Online tutoring or teaching | Medium | Low | Low |
| Selling print-on-demand products (e.g., t-shirts, mugs) | Medium | Low | Low |
| Dropshipping products through an e-commerce store | Medium | Low | Low |
| Photography services for events or stock photos | Medium | Low | Low |
| Carrying out affiliate marketing | Medium | Low | Low |
| Starting a blog or YouTube channel and monetizing through ads | Medium | Low | Low |
| Creating and selling digital products (e-books, templates, presets) | Medium | Low | Low |
| Selling second-hand books or vintage items online | Medium | Low | Low |
| Offering resume writing or career coaching services | Medium | Low | Low |
| Renting out camping spaces on your property | Medium | Low | Low |
| Launching an online course or membership site | Medium | Low | Low |
| Creating and selling custom jewelry or accessories | Medium | Low | Low |

"I have not failed. I've just found 10,000 ways that won't work"

Thomas A. Edison

| Side Hustle | Knowledge Needed | Money Needed | Profit Potential |
|---|---|---|---|
| Offering mobile phone repair services | Medium | Low | Low |
| Providing transcription services | Medium | Low | Low |
| Offering online language tutoring | Medium | Low | Low |
| Creating and selling personalized gifts | Medium | Low | Low |
| Running a local food delivery service | Medium | Low | Low |
| Providing IT support or computer repair services | Medium | Low | Low |
| Providing marketing or SEO services | Medium | Low | Low |
| Providing drone photography and videography services | Medium | Low | Low |
| Starting a specialty catering business (e.g., vegan, gluten-free) | Medium | Low | Low |
| Providing premium car detailing and protection services | Medium | Low | Low |
| Investing in dividend stocks or index funds | High | Low | High |
| Starting an online course or coaching business | High | Medium | High |
| Building and flipping websites | High | Medium | High |
| Developing and selling mobile apps | High | Medium | High |
| Creating and selling software or plugins | High | Medium | High |
| Providing specialized consulting services | High | Medium | High |
| Event planning and coordination services | High | Medium | High |
| Real estate investing (e.g., rental properties) | High | Medium | High |
| Trading cryptocurrencies or forex | High | Medium | High |
| Buying and selling domain names | High | Medium | High |
| Offering financial planning or investment advice | High | Medium | High |
| Running a subscription box service | High | Medium | High |
| Starting a food truck or catering business | High | Medium | High |
| Launching a podcast with sponsorships and ads | High | Medium | High |
| Importing and selling products from overseas | High | Medium | High |
| Providing home renovation or remodeling services | High | Medium | High |
| Providing interior design services | High | Medium | High |
| Developing and selling software as a service (SaaS) | High | Medium | High |
| Providing high-end wedding planning services | High | Medium | High |
| Offering home energy efficiency consulting | High | Medium | High |
| Starting a custom printing and merchandise business | High | Medium | High |
| Offering resume or audition tape review services | High | Medium | High |

"Wealth, like happiness, is never attained when sought after directly. It comes as a by-product of providing a useful service."

—Colonel Harlan Sanders, Founder of Kentucky Fried Chicken

## First considerations

Welcome to the world of side hustles, where you can turn your skills and passions into an exciting source of extra income! In this book, we will guide you through the process of finding the perfect side hustle that aligns with your interests and talents, ensuring that your journey to financial freedom is both enjoyable and rewarding.

## Choose a side hustle that matches your skills and interests.

Before embarking on any side hustle, it is crucial to identify activities that resonate with your strengths and bring you joy. By aligning your side hustle with your passions and expertise, you'll not only find it more fulfilling but also increase your chances of success. Whether you possess creative writing abilities, a flair for graphic design, or simply love spending time with pets, there's a side hustle waiting for you.

## Determine your time commitment.

Balancing a side hustle with your existing commitments can be both challenging and rewarding. To avoid burnout and maximize your productivity, assess how much time you can realistically dedicate to your side venture. By analyzing your daily schedule and recognizing potential time sinks, you'll find pockets of opportunity to invest in your side hustle, ultimately accelerating its growth.

## Make a strong business plan.

Turning your side hustle into a thriving business requires a solid plan of action. We'll walk you through the essential steps of crafting a business plan that outlines your goals, target customers, marketing strategies, and potential competition. By being adaptable and open to refining your plan as your side hustle evolves, you'll position yourself for long-term success.

## Outline of a general Business Plan.

I. Executive Summary

    a) Introduction to the side hustle idea

    b) Description of the business and its goals

    c) Overview of target market and customer demographics

    d) Summary of financial projections and earning goals

II. Business Description

    a) Explanation of the side hustle's products or service

    b) Unique selling points and competitive advantages

    c) Mission and vision statements

III. Market Analysis

    a) Overview of the industry and market trends

    b) Analysis of target market and customer needs

    c) Identification of key competitors and their strengths/weaknesses

a) Business structure (e.g., sole proprietorship, LLC)

b) Licensing and permits required

c) Intellectual property protection (if applicable)

d) Insurance and liability coverage

IX. Risk Analysis

a) Identification of potential risks and challenges

b) Mitigation strategies and risk management plans

c) Financial risk assessment and contingency planning

X. Conclusion

a) Recap of the side hustle concept and its value proposition

b) Affirmation of the business goals and growth potential

c) Commitment to execute the business plan effectively

## Figure out your earning goals.

Defining clear earning goals is vital to measuring your progress and staying motivated. Whether you aim to pay off debts, save for a dream vacation, or build a nest egg, you need to be realistic and set achievable financial milestones. Understanding the average earnings potential of your chosen side hustle will guide you in shaping your goals and celebrating each milestone reached.

## Familiarize yourself with the law.

As your side hustle gains momentum, understanding legal considerations becomes essential. From choosing the appropriate business structure, such as a sole proprietorship or LLC, to exploring insurance options for added protection, you will need the knowledge (or the professional services) to navigate the legal landscape confidently. Ensure peace of mind while focusing on your passion, knowing you've taken the necessary steps to safeguard yourself and your business.

As you embark on this side hustle journey, remember that success is a combination of determination, adaptability, and seizing opportunities. With the right knowledge and dedication, your side hustle can grow into something extraordinary – an exciting venture that enhances your life and empowers you to pursue your dreams. Let's dive into the world of side hustles and make your ambitions a reality!

## 01. Dog walking and pet sitting service

Starting a side hustle like a "Dog walking and pet sitting service" can be a rewarding venture for animal lovers and individuals looking to earn extra income. In this comprehensive guide, we will cover all the essential aspects you need to know before embarking on this side hustle. We'll explore the knowledge needed, money required to start, profit potential, pros and cons, dos and don'ts, and practical tips to help you launch and manage a successful dog walking and pet sitting service. Let's dive in!

Understanding Pet Behavior is crucial as a pet sitter and dog walker, you need to recognize signs of distress, anxiety, and illness in animals to provide appropriate care. Basic Pet Care tasks, including feeding, watering, administering medications (if required), and providing companionship, should be familiar to you. Acquire knowledge of basic pet first aid and safety measures to handle emergencies and keep pets secure during walks.

Ensure you understand any local regulations or licensing requirements related to operating a pet sitting business in your area. For the money needed, invest in pet care essentials such as leashes, harnesses, waste bags, food bowls, water containers, grooming tools, and pet toys. Consider getting liability insurance to protect yourself and your clients in case of any accidents or damages.

Allocate a budget for marketing efforts, such as creating business cards, flyers, and online advertising. If necessary, budget for transportation costs to reach clients' homes or pet sitting locations. The profit potential can vary based on factors like location, clientele, and the range of services offered. Expanding your client base through word-of-mouth, referrals, and online presence can significantly impact your earning potential.

Offering additional services like pet grooming, training, or pet photography can increase your revenue streams. Set competitive yet reasonable pricing that reflects your services' quality and value. On the pros side, you can choose your working hours and schedule to accommodate other commitments. The startup costs are relatively low compared to many other businesses.

For pet lovers, this side hustle allows for rewarding and enjoyable interactions with pets. However, on the cons side, pet care requires time and dedication, including evenings, weekends, and holidays. Handling animals comes with inherent risks, including bites and scratches. Demand may fluctuate based on holidays and vacation periods.

To make this side hustle a success, provide quality care and ensure the safety and well-being of the pets under your care. Foster trust and rapport with pet owners to secure repeat business. Maintain open and transparent communication with clients about their pets' activities and well-being.

Avoid taking on more clients than you can handle to provide quality care to each pet. Always prioritize the safety of the pets, yourself, and others during walks or pet sitting. Comply with any legal requirements or regulations related to pet sitting in your area.

Start locally by offering your services to friends, family, and neighbors to build your reputation and client base. Establish clear policies regarding pricing, cancellation, and any additional services. Use social media platforms, local community boards, and pet-related events to promote your services.

Maintain professionalism in all aspects of your business, including punctuality and communication. Consider offering related services like pet grooming or dog training to increase your earning potential. A dog walking and pet sitting service can be a fulfilling and profitable side hustle for those passionate about animals.

With the right knowledge, dedication, and attention to detail, you can create a successful venture that benefits both you and your furry clients. Prioritize pet safety, establish strong relationships with clients, and remain committed to delivering exceptional pet care. Good luck on your journey to becoming a trusted pet sitter and dog walker!

## 02. House cleaning and organization service

Starting a side hustle like a "House cleaning and organization service" can be a lucrative and fulfilling venture for individuals who enjoy keeping spaces tidy and organized. In this comprehensive guide, we will cover all the essential aspects you need to know before launching your house cleaning and organization service. We'll explore the knowledge needed, money required to start, profit potential, pros and cons, and dos and don'ts to help you build a successful side hustle. Let's get started!

Knowledge Needed: Familiarize yourself with effective cleaning techniques for various surfaces and materials, including hardwood floors, carpets, tiles, and different types of furniture. Understand different cleaning agents and their appropriate uses to ensure the safety of both your clients and their belongings. Learn practical organization strategies to maximize space and create functional and aesthetically pleasing environments. Develop efficient time management skills to complete cleaning and organization tasks promptly and meet clients' expectations. Enhance your customer service skills to communicate effectively with clients, understand their needs, and address any concerns. Acquire knowledge of marketing techniques to attract clients and build a strong customer base for your side hustle.

Money Needed: Budget for purchasing high-quality cleaning supplies, including cleaning agents, mops, brooms, microfiber cloths, and storage solutions. Invest in organizational tools like storage bins, shelves, and closet organizers to optimize spaces during organization services. Consider transportation costs if you need to travel to clients' locations for your services. Protect your business and clients by investing in liability insurance to cover any potential accidents or damages during your work.

Profit Potential: Set competitive yet profitable pricing for your services based on market rates and the quality of your work. Encourage repeat business by providing excellent service, fostering customer loyalty, and offering discounts for regular clients. Satisfied clients can be your best promoters, leading to a steady stream of new customers through word-of-mouth referrals. Explore upselling opportunities by offering additional services like deep cleaning or specialized organization solutions for higher profits.

Pros: Enjoy the flexibility of setting your own schedule and working hours that align with your existing commitments. Compared to other businesses, the startup costs for a house cleaning and organization service are relatively low. Experience the satisfaction of transforming cluttered spaces into clean, organized, and functional areas for your clients. There is a constant demand for house cleaning and organization services, providing ample opportunities for business growth.

Cons: House cleaning and organization services require physical exertion, which can be tiring for some individuals. Accidents or damages during your work can potentially lead to liability issues and financial implications. The demand for your services may vary based on seasonal factors and holidays, leading to fluctuations in income. Meeting varying client expectations and preferences can be challenging and may require adaptability in your approach.

Do's: Set clear policies regarding pricing, cancellation, and scope of services to avoid misunderstandings with clients. Maintain open communication with clients to understand their specific needs and deliver tailored services. Focus on providing high-quality cleaning and organization services to build a strong reputation and secure repeat clients. Utilize online platforms, social media, and local advertising to promote your services and reach potential clients.

Don'ts: Avoid making unrealistic promises to clients that you cannot fulfill, as it can harm your reputation. Prioritize safety during your work to prevent accidents and minimize potential risks to you and your clients. Ensure your pricing reflects the value and quality of your work, avoiding undercharging and diminishing your profits. Avoid taking on more clients or projects than you can handle, as it may compromise the quality of your services.

In conclusion, a house cleaning and organization service can be a profitable and fulfilling side hustle for individuals with the right knowledge, skills, and dedication. By understanding cleaning techniques, organization strategies, and customer service, you can deliver exceptional services that lead to satisfied clients and repeat business. Be mindful of the startup costs, profit potential, and seasonal fluctuations, and always prioritize safety, quality, and clear communication with your clients. With diligence and professionalism, you can turn your passion for cleaning and organization into a successful side hustle venture.

## 03. Lawn mowing and gardening service

Starting a side hustle like a "Lawn mowing and gardening service" can be a rewarding and profitable venture for individuals who enjoy working outdoors and have a passion for gardening. In this comprehensive guide, we will cover all the essential aspects you need to know before launching your lawn mowing and gardening service. We'll explore the knowledge needed, money required to start, profit potential, pros and cons, and dos and don'ts to help you build a successful side hustle. Let's dive in!

Knowledge Needed: Familiarize yourself with various lawn mowing techniques, including how to mow different types of grass and handle uneven terrains. Understand the basics of lawn care, such as proper watering, fertilization, and weed control. Learn about common gardening tasks, like planting, pruning, and pest management. Acquire knowledge of different plant species and their specific care requirements. Educate yourself on safety practices while using lawn mowing equipment and handling garden tools. Enhance your communication skills to effectively interact with clients and understand their gardening needs.

Money Needed: Budget for purchasing lawn mowing equipment, including lawn mowers, trimmers, and leaf blowers. Allocate funds for gardening tools, such as shovels, rakes, pruners, and watering equipment. Consider transportation costs if you need to travel to clients' locations for your services. Set aside a budget for marketing and advertising efforts to promote your lawn mowing and gardening service. Consider investing in liability insurance to protect your business and clients in case of accidents or damages during your work.

Profit Potential: Set competitive pricing for your lawn mowing and gardening services based on the size of the lawn or garden and the scope of work. Encourage repeat business by providing excellent service and building strong relationships with clients. Leverage word-of-mouth referrals from satisfied customers to attract new clients. Offer additional services, such as landscaping or garden design, to increase your revenue streams.

Pros: Enjoy the flexibility of setting your own work schedule and hours to accommodate other commitments. Experience the satisfaction of transforming overgrown lawns and gardens into well-maintained and beautiful spaces. Low startup costs compared to many other businesses, making it an accessible side hustle option. High demand for lawn mowing and gardening services, especially during spring and summer, providing a steady flow of potential clients.

Cons: Physical demands of lawn mowing and gardening tasks may be strenuous and tiring for some individuals. Weather conditions can impact your work schedule, especially during extreme heat or rainy periods. Seasonal fluctuations in demand may affect your income during slower months. Competing with other lawn care and gardening services in your area can be challenging.

Do's: Set clear pricing and service agreements with clients to avoid misunderstandings. Offer personalized and tailored services based on each client's lawn and garden needs. Focus on providing high-quality work to build a positive reputation and secure repeat business. Invest in reliable lawn mowing equipment and gardening tools to ensure efficient and effective services.

Don'ts: Avoid overbooking yourself to maintain the quality of your work and meet clients' expectations. Don't neglect safety precautions while using lawn mowing equipment and garden tools. Avoid making unrealistic promises to clients regarding the results of your lawn mowing and gardening services. Don't overlook the importance of marketing and promoting your services to reach potential clients.

In conclusion, a lawn mowing and gardening service can be a fulfilling and profitable side hustle for individuals with a passion for outdoor work and gardening. By acquiring the necessary knowledge and skills, setting competitive pricing, and delivering exceptional services, you can establish a successful side business. Be mindful of the startup costs, profit potential, and seasonal fluctuations, and prioritize safety and customer satisfaction in your lawn mowing and gardening endeavors. With dedication and professionalism, you can turn your love for landscaping into a thriving side hustle venture.

## 04. Car washing and detailing service

Starting a side hustle like a "Car washing and detailing service" can be a profitable and rewarding venture for individuals who have a passion for cars and enjoy making vehicles look their best. In this comprehensive guide, we will cover all the essential aspects you need to know before launching your car washing and detailing service. We'll explore the knowledge needed, money required to start, profit potential, pros and cons, and dos and don'ts to help you build a successful side hustle. Let's delve into the details!

Knowledge Needed: Familiarize yourself with different car washing techniques, including hand washing, pressure washing, and foam washing. Understand the proper use of car cleaning products, such as soaps, shampoos, waxes, and polishes. Learn about interior detailing, which includes cleaning and conditioning car seats, carpets, and other surfaces. Acquire knowledge of exterior detailing, such as buffing, clay bar treatment, and paint correction. Educate yourself on safety practices while working with cleaning chemicals and car detailing equipment. Enhance your customer service skills to interact effectively with clients and understand their car care needs.

Money Needed: Budget for car washing and detailing supplies, including car wash mitts, microfiber towels, detailing brushes, and applicators. Allocate funds for high-quality car cleaning products and detailing chemicals. Consider investing in professional-grade car detailing equipment, such as a pressure washer, steam cleaner, and polishing machine. Set aside a budget for marketing and advertising efforts to promote your car washing and detailing service. Factor in transportation costs if you need to travel to clients' locations for your services.

Profit Potential: Set competitive pricing for your car washing and detailing services based on the size and condition of the vehicle and the scope of work. Offer various detailing packages to cater to different customer preferences and budgets. Encourage repeat business by providing exceptional service and building strong relationships with clients. Leverage positive customer reviews and referrals to attract new customers. Explore additional revenue streams, such as offering mobile car detailing services or partnering with local car dealerships.

Pros: Enjoy the flexibility of setting your own work schedule and hours to fit your lifestyle. Fulfillment in seeing the immediate transformation of cars after detailing, leaving clients satisfied. Low startup costs compared to many other businesses, making it an accessible side hustle option. High demand for car washing and detailing services, with potential for repeat business from loyal customers.

Cons: Physical demands of car detailing tasks may be strenuous and require prolonged periods of standing and bending. Weather conditions can impact your work schedule, especially for outdoor car detailing. Intense competition in the car detailing industry may pose challenges in attracting new customers. Time-consuming nature of detailed car cleaning may limit the number of cars you can service in a day.

Do's: Offer personalized and tailored car detailing services based on each client's needs and preferences. Focus on providing high-quality work and attention to detail to build a positive reputation. Invest in professional-grade car detailing equipment and high-quality cleaning products for excellent results. Create a strong online presence through social media and a professional website to showcase your services and attract customers.

Don'ts: Avoid using harsh cleaning chemicals that may damage car surfaces or harm the environment. Don't overbook yourself to ensure you can deliver high-quality detailing services to each customer. Avoid making promises or guarantees regarding the results of car detailing, as each vehicle's condition may vary. Don't neglect customer service; excellent communication and attentiveness to clients' concerns are vital for a successful car washing and detailing service.

In conclusion, a car washing and detailing service can be a lucrative side hustle for individuals passionate about cars and detailing. By acquiring the necessary knowledge and skills, providing exceptional service, and investing in quality equipment and products, you can build a successful car detailing business. Be mindful of the startup costs, profit potential, and challenges that come with the industry, and prioritize safety, customer satisfaction, and professionalism in your car washing and detailing endeavors. With dedication and a commitment to excellence, your car detailing side hustle can thrive and become a satisfying and profitable venture.

## 05. Renting out a room or property on Airbnb

Starting a side hustle like "Renting out a room or property on Airbnb" can be an excellent way to generate additional income by leveraging your spare space or property. In this comprehensive guide, we will cover all the essential aspects you need to know before embarking on this venture. We'll explore the knowledge needed, money required to start, profit potential, pros and cons, and dos and don'ts to help you build a successful Airbnb rental business. Let's dive in!

Knowledge Needed: Familiarize yourself with the Airbnb platform, including how to create a listing, manage bookings, and communicate with guests. Understand local regulations and legal requirements for short-term rentals in your area. Acquire knowledge of effective property management, such as housekeeping, maintenance, and responding to guest inquiries promptly. Learn about hospitality and customer service to ensure a positive guest experience. Educate yourself on pricing strategies, market trends, and competition to set competitive rates.

Money Needed: Budget for initial setup costs, including furnishing, decorating, and equipping the rental space with essential amenities. Allocate funds for professional photography to showcase your property attractively. Consider investing in property improvements to enhance its appeal to potential guests. Set aside a budget for marketing and promotion to increase the visibility of your listing. Factor in ongoing expenses, such as utilities, cleaning services, and maintenance.

Profit Potential: Set competitive pricing for your rental based on factors like location, amenities, and seasonal demand. Maximize profits by offering additional services or experiences to guests, such as guided tours or cooking classes. Encourage repeat business by providing exceptional hospitality and building positive guest reviews. Leverage peak travel seasons and local events to increase booking rates. Consider long-term rental arrangements or corporate bookings for stable and consistent income.

Pros: Generate passive income by renting out your room or property when it's not in use. Flexible work schedule, allowing you to manage bookings and guests based on your availability. Opportunity to meet people from diverse backgrounds and cultures through hosting. Potential for higher earnings during peak travel seasons and special events. Opportunity to transform unused spaces into income-generating assets.

Cons: Potential for occasional vacancies, affecting income during slower booking periods. Time-consuming nature of guest communication, check-ins, and housekeeping tasks. Risk of property damage or negative guest experiences, requiring immediate attention and resolution. Compliance with local regulations and taxes can be complex and time-consuming. Competition from other Airbnb listings and traditional accommodation options in your area.

Do's: Create a detailed and accurate listing with high-quality photos to attract potential guests. Set clear house rules and expectations to ensure a positive guest experience. Provide essential amenities and thoughtful touches to enhance guest comfort. Respond promptly to guest inquiries and messages to maintain positive communication. Be hospitable and accommodating to create a welcoming atmosphere for guests.

Don'ts: Don't overprice your rental, as it may deter potential guests and lead to longer vacancies. Avoid neglecting property maintenance and cleanliness, as it can lead to negative reviews. Don't oversell or misrepresent your rental; be honest about the space and amenities. Avoid discriminatory practices; ensure fairness and inclusivity in accepting guests. Don't neglect your responsibilities as a host; prioritize guest satisfaction and timely communication.

In conclusion, renting out a room or property on Airbnb can be a profitable and rewarding side hustle with the right knowledge and approach. By understanding the Airbnb platform, adhering to local regulations, and providing exceptional hospitality, you can create a successful rental business. Be mindful of the initial setup costs, ongoing expenses, and potential challenges associated with hosting guests. With careful planning, attention to guest needs, and dedication to maintaining a positive guest experience, your Airbnb rental side hustle can thrive and become a valuable source of additional income.

## 06. Running errands for busy individuals

Starting a side hustle like "Running errands for busy individuals" can be a rewarding and flexible way to earn extra income by helping others manage their busy schedules.

In this comprehensive guide, we will cover all the essential aspects you need to know before launching your errand running service. We'll explore the knowledge needed, money required to start, profit potential, pros and cons, and dos and don'ts to help you build a successful side hustle. Let's get started!

Knowledge Needed: Familiarize yourself with various types of errands that individuals may need assistance with, such as grocery shopping, dry cleaning pickups, and mail handling. Understand the importance of punctuality and reliability in fulfilling clients' errands. Acquire knowledge of efficient time management to handle multiple errands and meet deadlines. Enhance your communication and organizational skills to effectively coordinate with clients and understand their specific needs. Learn about the local area and various services available to facilitate errand running.

Money Needed: Budget for transportation costs, including fuel or public transportation fees, to travel to different locations for errands. Allocate funds for any necessary equipment or tools needed to fulfill specific errands. Set aside a budget for marketing and promotion to attract potential clients to your service. Consider obtaining insurance coverage to protect yourself and your clients in case of any accidents or incidents during errand running.

Profit Potential: Set competitive pricing for your errand running services based on the type and complexity of the errands. Offer various service packages to cater to different clients' needs and budgets. Encourage repeat business by providing reliable and efficient service to build trust and loyalty with clients. Leverage word-of-mouth referrals from satisfied clients to expand your customer base. Consider partnering with local businesses or organizations to offer specialized errand services for additional revenue streams.

Pros: Enjoy the flexibility of setting your own work schedule and availability to fit your other commitments. Fulfillment in helping busy individuals manage their daily tasks and reducing their stress. Low startup costs compared to many other businesses, making it an accessible side hustle option. High demand for errand running services, especially in urban areas with busy professionals and seniors. Opportunity to establish long-term client relationships and create a positive impact on their lives.

Cons: Physical demands of running errands may involve carrying heavy items or standing for extended periods. Time constraints and unpredictable schedules may require adaptability and time management skills. Competition from other errand running services and gig economy platforms may affect your market presence. Potential challenges in coordinating multiple errands and handling clients' changing requirements. Liability risks associated with handling clients' personal belongings or sensitive information.

Do's: Communicate clearly with clients to understand their errand needs and expectations. Be punctual and reliable in fulfilling clients' errands to build trust and satisfaction. Keep accurate records of clients' requests and errand details for efficient service. Offer personalized and attentive service to create a positive and memorable experience for clients.

Market your services effectively through social media, local advertising, and word-of-mouth referrals.

Don'ts: Don't overpromise on your ability to fulfill certain errands if you're unsure about completing them successfully. Avoid neglecting client communication; respond promptly to inquiries and updates. Don't forget to factor in travel time and logistics when scheduling multiple errands. Avoid neglecting your own well-being; ensure you have adequate breaks and rest to maintain high-quality service. Don't overlook potential safety risks during errand running; prioritize caution and care while handling clients' requests.

In conclusion, running errands for busy individuals can be a fulfilling and profitable side hustle for individuals with strong organizational and communication skills. By understanding clients' needs, offering reliable service, and managing time efficiently, you can build a successful errand running business. Be mindful of the initial expenses, competition, and potential challenges associated with this side hustle. With dedication, attention to detail, and a commitment to exceptional service, your errand running side hustle can thrive and become a valuable resource for those in need of assistance with their daily tasks.

## 07. Selling handmade crafts on Etsy

Starting a side hustle like "Selling handmade crafts on Etsy" can be a fulfilling and creative way to turn your crafting skills into a profitable venture. In this comprehensive guide, we will cover all the essential aspects you need to know before launching your Etsy shop. We'll explore the knowledge needed, money required to start, profit potential, pros and cons, and dos and don'ts to help you build a successful side hustle. Let's delve into the details!

Knowledge Needed: Familiarize yourself with the Etsy platform, including how to set up a shop, create listings, and manage orders. Understand the basics of crafting techniques and materials to create high-quality handmade products. Acquire knowledge of photography and product styling to showcase your crafts attractively. Learn about branding and marketing to effectively promote your Etsy shop. Educate yourself on pricing strategies, market trends, and competition to set competitive prices for your crafts.

Money Needed: Budget for crafting materials and supplies needed to create your handmade products. Allocate funds for professional product photography and branding materials to establish a strong shop presence. Consider Etsy fees, which include listing fees, transaction fees, and payment processing fees. Set aside a budget for marketing and promotion to increase the visibility of your Etsy shop. Factor in shipping costs and packaging materials for delivering your crafts to customers.

Profit Potential: Set competitive pricing for your handmade crafts based on factors like production cost, time invested, and market demand. Offer various products or customizations to cater to different customer preferences and budgets. Encourage repeat business by providing excellent customer service and building a positive reputation. Leverage customer reviews and word-of-mouth referrals to attract new customers. Consider offering wholesale or bulk purchase options for additional revenue streams.

Pros: Flexibility to manage your Etsy shop and create crafts based on your own schedule. Fulfillment in seeing customers appreciate and enjoy your handmade products. Low startup costs compared to many other businesses, making it an accessible side hustle option. Opportunity to tap into a global marketplace and reach a wide range of customers. Potential for growth and expansion by introducing new product lines or collaborating with other sellers.

Cons: Time-consuming nature of crafting, listing, and managing an Etsy shop, especially during busy periods. Competition from other Etsy sellers and handmade crafters may affect your shop visibility. Need for continuous innovation and creativity to stand out in a saturated market. Financial risk of slow sales or unsold inventory, especially during low-demand periods. Responsibility for customer service, including handling inquiries, refunds, and shipping issues.

Do's: Create high-quality and unique handmade crafts that align with your artistic vision and customer preferences. Invest in professional product photography to showcase your crafts attractively. Provide accurate and detailed product descriptions to inform customers about your crafts. Offer excellent customer service, including prompt responses and timely order fulfillment. Build a strong brand identity and shop presence through consistent branding and marketing efforts.

Don'ts: Avoid neglecting the importance of high-quality craftsmanship in your handmade products. Don't overprice your crafts; consider production costs and market demand when setting prices. Avoid using copyright-infringing materials or designs in your crafts to maintain ethical business practices. Don't ignore customer feedback and reviews; use them to improve your products and customer experience. Avoid rushing or sacrificing quality to meet high demand; prioritize craftsmanship and customer satisfaction.

In conclusion, selling handmade crafts on Etsy can be a rewarding and profitable side hustle for individuals with crafting skills and a passion for creativity. By understanding the Etsy platform, creating high-quality crafts, and engaging in effective marketing, you can build a successful Etsy shop. Be mindful of the initial expenses, competition, and time commitment associated with running an Etsy shop. With dedication, artistic flair, and a commitment to excellent customer service, your Etsy handmade crafts side hustle can flourish and become a thriving and satisfying business venture.

## 08. Reselling thrift store finds online

Starting a side hustle like "Reselling thrift store finds online" can be a lucrative and enjoyable way to earn extra income by finding hidden gems and selling them at a profit. In this comprehensive guide, we will cover all the essential aspects you need to know before diving into the world of online thrift store reselling. We'll explore the knowledge needed, money required to start, profit potential, pros and cons, and dos and don'ts to help you build a successful side hustle. Let's delve into the details!

Knowledge Needed: Familiarize yourself with various thrift stores and secondhand markets in your area to source potential items for reselling. Acquire knowledge of popular and trending items that have high resale value. Understand different online selling platforms, such as eBay, Poshmark, and Depop, to choose the most suitable platform for your business. Educate yourself on pricing strategies, shipping options, and customer service to create a positive buying experience for your customers. Enhance your negotiation skills to get the best deals on thrift store finds.

Money Needed: Budget for purchasing thrift store items and initial inventory to kickstart your online reselling venture. Allocate funds for cleaning and refurbishing any items that may need some TLC (Tender Loving Care: giving special attention and care to clean and improve the condition of the thrift store items before putting them up for sale) before listing them for sale. Set aside a budget for packaging and shipping materials to ensure secure and professional delivery to customers. Consider online selling platform fees, which may include listing fees and transaction fees. Factor in marketing and promotional costs to increase the visibility of your online store.

Profit Potential: Set competitive pricing for your thrift store finds based on factors like item condition, rarity, and market demand. Offer various sales and promotions to attract potential buyers and encourage repeat business. Encourage positive customer reviews and feedback to build trust and credibility in your online store. Leverage social media and online marketing to reach a broader audience and drive sales. Consider bundling or offering discounted shipping for multiple items to increase the average order value.

Pros: Enjoy the thrill of hunting for unique and valuable items in thrift stores and flea markets. Flexibility to set your own work hours and manage your online reselling business from anywhere. Low startup costs compared to many other businesses, making it an accessible side hustle option. Opportunity to turn your passion for thrifting into a profitable and sustainable income stream. Potential for growth and expansion by diversifying your product offerings and establishing a loyal customer base.

Cons: Time-consuming nature of sourcing, listing, and managing an online reselling store, especially during peak seasons. Competition from other online resellers and thrift store enthusiasts may affect your sales. Need for continuous research and market monitoring to stay up-to-date with trends and pricing. Financial risk of investing in thrift store items that may not sell or generate the expected profit. Responsibility for customer service, including handling inquiries, returns, and shipping issues.

Do's: Inspect thrift store items carefully to ensure they are in good condition and suitable for resale. Take high-quality and clear photographs of your items to showcase them attractively online. Write detailed and accurate product descriptions to inform buyers about the items' condition and features. Offer competitive shipping options and promptly ship out orders to maintain customer satisfaction. Engage with customers and respond to inquiries or feedback promptly to build trust and rapport.

Don'ts: Avoid purchasing damaged or heavily worn items that may not be salvageable or marketable. Don't overprice your thrift store finds; research market values and be competitive in your pricing. Refrain from using stock photos or misleading images; provide genuine photos of the actual items for sale. Don't neglect marketing efforts; promote your online store through social media and relevant online communities. Avoid neglecting your online presence; update your store regularly with new listings and remove sold items promptly.

In conclusion, reselling thrift store finds online can be a profitable and enjoyable side hustle for individuals with an eye for valuable and unique items. By understanding online selling platforms, sourcing high-quality items, and providing excellent customer service, you can build a successful online reselling business. Be mindful of the initial expenses, competition, and time commitment associated with running an online store. With dedication, research, and a commitment to customer satisfaction, your thrift store reselling side hustle can flourish and become a rewarding and profitable business venture.

## 09. Participating in online surveys or market research

Before diving into the side hustle of "Participating in online surveys or market research," it is essential to understand the various aspects involved to make informed decisions for a successful venture. In this comprehensive guide, we will explore the knowledge needed, money required to start, profit potential, pros and cons, and do's and don'ts to help you navigate the world of online surveys and market research. Let's get started!

Knowledge Needed: Familiarize yourself with reputable and legitimate online survey and market research platforms. Understand the types of surveys and research studies conducted, ranging from consumer opinions to product feedback. Acquire knowledge of data privacy and protection regulations to ensure your personal information is safeguarded while participating in surveys. Learn how to effectively manage your time and prioritize survey opportunities to maximize your earnings. Enhance your communication skills to provide honest and valuable feedback in surveys and research studies.

Money Needed: Participating in online surveys and market research generally does not require any initial investment. Reputable survey platforms are free to join and offer opportunities to earn money or rewards by sharing your opinions. However, you may need to allocate time and effort to complete surveys regularly to accumulate earnings or rewards.

Profit Potential: The profit potential in online surveys and market research can vary based on factors such as the number of surveys available, your eligibility for specific surveys, and the rewards or compensation offered for each survey completed. Earnings from online surveys may range from a few dollars to a significant amount per survey, depending on the complexity and length of the study. Some platforms offer additional incentives, such as gift cards, product samples, or entries into prize draws.

Pros: Flexibility to participate in surveys from the comfort of your home or on-the-go, allowing you to set your own schedule. Low barriers to entry, as most survey platforms are open to anyone with internet access. The opportunity to share your opinions and influence the development of products and services. Access to rewards or compensation for sharing your time and insights. Some survey platforms offer referral programs, allowing you to earn additional rewards by inviting friends and family to join.

Cons: Earnings from online surveys may not replace a full-time income and are more suitable as a supplementary income source. Not all survey platforms are legitimate, so it's crucial to research and choose reputable ones. Some surveys may have eligibility criteria, and you may not qualify for every survey opportunity. Participating in surveys can be time-consuming, and the compensation may not always match the effort required. Survey opportunities may fluctuate, resulting in inconsistent earning opportunities.

Do's: Join reputable and well-established online survey and market research platforms with positive user reviews. Provide honest and thoughtful responses in surveys to contribute valuable insights. Regularly check your survey dashboard for available opportunities to maximize your earnings. Set realistic expectations for your survey earnings and consider it a supplementary income source. Stay consistent and patient as it may take time to accumulate earnings or rewards.

Don'ts: Avoid signing up for survey platforms that require upfront fees or promise unrealistic earnings. Don't rush through surveys without providing genuine feedback, as this may affect your eligibility for future opportunities. Avoid sharing personal or sensitive information in surveys unless you trust the platform's data privacy policies. Don't rely solely on online surveys as a primary source of income, as earnings can be inconsistent.

In conclusion, participating in online surveys or market research can be a convenient and accessible side hustle for individuals who want to share their opinions and earn extra income or rewards. By understanding reputable survey platforms, managing your time effectively, and providing genuine feedback, you can make the most of this side hustle. Be mindful of the potential earnings, eligibility criteria, and time commitment associated with online surveys. With a thoughtful and patient approach, your online survey and market research side hustle can be a rewarding and valuable way to contribute your insights while earning some extra rewards or compensation.

## 10. Renting out your car or unused parking space

Before delving into the side hustle of "Renting out your car or unused parking space," it is crucial to understand the various aspects involved to make informed decisions and ensure a successful venture. In this comprehensive guide, we will explore the knowledge needed, money required to start, profit potential, pros and cons, and do's and don'ts to help you navigate the world of car and parking space rentals. Let's get started!

Knowledge Needed: Familiarize yourself with the local regulations and laws regarding car rentals and parking space usage in your area. Understand the insurance requirements and coverage options when renting out your car to ensure adequate protection for you and your renters. Acquire knowledge of your car's market value and condition to set appropriate rental rates. Learn about the different car-sharing or peer-to-peer platforms available to list your car for rental. Educate yourself on customer service and communication skills to interact effectively with potential renters.

Money Needed: Budget for maintenance and upkeep of your car to ensure it is in optimal condition for rental. Allocate funds for professional cleaning and detailing of your car before listing it for rental. Consider insurance costs and potential premium increases associated with using your car for rental purposes. If you are renting out your parking space, allocate funds for any necessary improvements or signage to make it attractive and accessible to renters. Set aside a budget for marketing and promotion to increase visibility and attract potential renters.

Profit Potential: The profit potential in renting out your car or parking space can vary based on factors such as location, demand, and rental rates. Earnings from car rentals may range from a percentage of the rental fees to a fixed amount per day. If you live in a high-demand area with limited parking space, renting out your parking spot can be a lucrative source of passive income. Profit potential can be maximized by offering competitive rates, providing excellent customer service, and attracting repeat renters.

Pros: Opportunity to generate passive income by utilizing your car or unused parking space. Flexibility to set your own rental schedule and availability. Potential to earn more during peak travel seasons or special events. Contributing to sustainability and reducing environmental impact by promoting car-sharing practices. The possibility of meeting new people and building connections through the rental process.

Cons: Risk of wear and tear on your car from frequent rentals, leading to potential maintenance costs. The responsibility of maintaining insurance coverage and dealing with potential insurance claims in case of accidents. Potential liability concerns if your car is involved in an accident while rented. The need to carefully screen potential renters to ensure responsible and reliable individuals use your car. If renting out your parking space, it may not be available for personal use during rental periods.

Do's: Thoroughly research and choose reputable car-sharing or parking space rental platforms with positive user reviews. Clean and maintain your car regularly to ensure it is in excellent condition for renters. Set clear and competitive rental rates based on the market value of your car and local demand. Ensure your car insurance policy covers rental usage and consider additional coverage options for added protection. Communicate promptly and clearly with potential renters, addressing any questions or concerns they may have.

Don'ts: Avoid overlooking insurance requirements and coverage limitations when renting out your car. Don't neglect necessary maintenance or repairs on your car, as it may lead to negative reviews from renters. Avoid overbooking your car or parking space, which can lead to dissatisfaction and negative feedback. Don't rent out your car or parking space to individuals who do not meet your screening criteria or seem unreliable. Avoid providing inaccurate or misleading information about your car or parking space in rental listings.

In conclusion, renting out your car or unused parking space can be a profitable and flexible side hustle for individuals looking to generate passive income. By understanding the local regulations, insurance requirements, and market demand, you can make informed decisions for a successful rental venture. Be mindful of the initial expenses, maintenance costs, and potential liabilities associated with car and parking space rentals. With proper planning, clear communication, and a commitment to providing excellent service, your car or parking space rental side hustle can thrive and become a valuable source of additional income.

## 11. Data entry and virtual assisting services

Before embarking on a side hustle in "Data entry and virtual assisting services," it is essential to gain a comprehensive understanding of the various aspects involved to ensure a successful venture. In this comprehensive guide, we will explore the knowledge needed, money required to start, profit potential, pros and cons, and do's and don'ts to help you navigate the world of data entry and virtual assisting. Let's delve into the details!

Knowledge Needed: Familiarize yourself with various data entry and virtual assisting tasks, such as data input, spreadsheet management, email correspondence, scheduling, and customer support. Acquire proficiency in computer applications, such as Microsoft Office Suite (Word, Excel, PowerPoint), Google Workspace, and productivity tools. Learn about time management and organizational skills to efficiently handle multiple tasks and deadlines. Enhance your communication and interpersonal skills to provide excellent virtual assistance to clients. Stay updated on technological advancements and software tools relevant to data entry and virtual assisting.

Money Needed: Data entry and virtual assisting services typically have low startup costs. Budget for a reliable computer or laptop with adequate processing power and memory to handle various tasks efficiently. Allocate funds for high-speed internet connection to ensure seamless communication with clients. Consider investing in productivity software or tools to streamline data entry and virtual assistance tasks. Set aside a budget for marketing and promotion to attract potential clients and grow your client base.

Profit Potential: The profit potential in data entry and virtual assisting services can vary based on factors such as experience, expertise, and client demand. Earnings from data entry tasks may be based on an hourly rate or per project basis. Virtual assistants can charge hourly rates or offer packages for specific services. Profit potential can be maximized by offering specialized services, building a strong client portfolio, and delivering high-quality work that fosters repeat business and referrals.

Pros: Flexibility to work from home or any location with an internet connection, allowing you to set your own schedule. Low barriers to entry, as data entry and virtual assisting services require minimal upfront investment. The opportunity to work with diverse clients and industries, providing exposure to various tasks and responsibilities. Potential to expand services and skillsets, offering a range of virtual assistance solutions. The ability to establish long-term relationships with clients, fostering trust and loyalty.

Cons: Data entry tasks can be repetitive and monotonous, requiring focus and attention to detail. The competition in the virtual assisting industry can be high, requiring efforts to stand out and attract clients. Virtual assistants may encounter challenging clients or deadlines that demand efficient problem-solving skills. The potential for inconsistent workloads, with busy and slow periods depending on client demand. The responsibility of managing administrative tasks, such as billing and invoicing.

Do's: Offer reliable and accurate data entry services to maintain client satisfaction and trust. Set clear communication channels and respond promptly to client inquiries and requests. Practice time management and organizational skills to meet deadlines and handle multiple tasks efficiently. Continuously update your knowledge and skills to offer valuable and up-to-date virtual assisting services. Provide exceptional customer service and prioritize client needs to build strong, long-term relationships.

Don'ts: Avoid underestimating the time and effort required for data entry tasks; allocate adequate time for each project. Don't overlook the importance of data security and confidentiality when handling sensitive information. Avoid overcommitting to multiple projects without considering your capacity to deliver quality work. Don't neglect marketing efforts; promote your data entry and virtual assisting services to attract clients. Avoid taking on tasks outside your expertise or capabilities; focus on offering services you excel in.

In conclusion, data entry and virtual assisting services can be a rewarding and flexible side hustle for individuals with strong organizational and computer skills. By understanding the tasks involved, maintaining data accuracy, and providing excellent virtual assistance, you can establish a successful side business. Be mindful of the initial expenses, competition, and time management associated with data entry and virtual assisting. With dedication, continuous improvement, and a commitment to client satisfaction, your data entry and virtual assisting side hustle can flourish and become a valuable source of additional income.

## 12. House or pet sitting for neighbors or friends

Before venturing into a side hustle like "House or pet sitting for neighbors or friends," it is essential to gain a comprehensive understanding of the various aspects involved to ensure a successful and rewarding experience. In this comprehensive guide, we will explore the knowledge needed, money required to start, profit potential, pros and cons, and do's and don'ts to help you navigate the world of house and pet sitting. Let's delve into the details!

Knowledge Needed: Familiarize yourself with the responsibilities and expectations of house and pet sitting, which may include caring for pets, ensuring home security, and handling household tasks. Acquire knowledge of pet care, such as feeding schedules, exercise routines, and administering medications if required. Learn about emergency protocols and contacts in case of unforeseen situations. Familiarize yourself with the local regulations and laws related to house and pet sitting, especially if you are taking care of pets that require special permits or licenses.

Money Needed: House and pet sitting typically do not require significant initial investment. However, budget for transportation costs if you need to commute to the neighbor's or friend's home for the sitting assignment. Consider any expenses related to pet care, such as purchasing pet food or supplies, which may be reimbursed by the pet owner. If you offer additional services, such as watering plants or collecting mail, allocate funds for any required materials or resources.

Profit Potential: The profit potential in house and pet sitting can vary based on factors such as the duration of the sitting assignments and the services you offer. House sitters may charge a daily or weekly rate, while pet sitters may charge per visit or per day. Profit potential can be maximized by building a reputation for reliability and trustworthiness, which can lead to repeat business and referrals. Additionally, offering additional services, such as plant care or mail collection, can increase your earnings.

Pros: Flexibility to choose house and pet sitting assignments that fit your schedule and availability. The opportunity to spend time with pets and enjoy their companionship without the long-term commitment of pet ownership. House sitters may have the chance to experience living in different neighborhoods or even traveling to new locations for sitting assignments. The potential to build strong bonds with neighbors and friends through providing a valuable service. The satisfaction of knowing that you are helping pet owners ensure their pets' well-being and providing peace of mind during their absence.

Cons: House and pet sitting may require flexibility in your own schedule, especially if you have other commitments or responsibilities. The responsibility of caring for someone else's home and pets, which may include handling emergencies or unexpected situations. The potential for encountering challenging or unfamiliar pets that may require additional care and attention. The need to be highly responsible and reliable, as pet owners are entrusting you with the care of their beloved pets and homes. The possibility of facing conflicts or misunderstandings with neighbors or friends if expectations are not clearly communicated.

Do's: Establish clear expectations and responsibilities with the neighbor or friend before starting the house or pet sitting assignment. Gather all necessary information, including emergency contacts, pet care routines, and house rules, to ensure a smooth experience. Communicate regularly with the pet owner during the sitting assignment to provide updates and address any concerns. Respect the privacy and property of the neighbor or friend while house sitting. Ensure the safety and well-being of pets by following their regular routines and providing adequate care.

Don'ts: Avoid taking on house or pet sitting assignments that you are not comfortable or familiar with, especially if you lack experience with specific pets or responsibilities. Don't neglect the care and attention required for the pets you are responsible for; their well-being is of utmost importance. Avoid leaving the house unattended for extended periods during the sitting assignment to maintain security. Don't make assumptions about the pet's needs or behaviors; always communicate with the owner to understand their specific care requirements. Avoid making changes to the pet's diet or routine without the owner's consent.

In conclusion, house or pet sitting for neighbors or friends can be a rewarding and enjoyable side hustle, offering the chance to care for pets and homes while building meaningful connections with your community. By understanding the responsibilities involved, establishing clear expectations, and providing reliable care, you can offer a valuable service and create positive experiences for both the pet owners and the pets. Be mindful of the responsibilities, flexibility, and communication required for successful house and pet sitting. With dedication and a commitment to pet and homeowner satisfaction, your house and pet sitting side hustle can flourish and become a trusted and sought-after service in your neighborhood or circle of friends.

## 13. Starting a neighborhood cleaning service

Before embarking on a side hustle like "Starting a neighborhood cleaning service," it is essential to equip yourself with a comprehensive understanding of the various aspects involved to ensure a successful and profitable venture. In this comprehensive guide, we will explore the knowledge needed, money required to start, profit potential, pros and cons, and do's and don'ts to help you navigate the world of neighborhood cleaning services. Let's delve into the details!

Knowledge Needed: Familiarize yourself with different cleaning techniques and equipment for various surfaces and spaces. Acquire knowledge of eco-friendly and safe cleaning products to cater to environmentally conscious clients.

Understand the importance of time management and efficiency in cleaning operations to provide timely and satisfactory services. Learn about customer service and communication skills to address client needs and build lasting relationships. Educate yourself on local regulations and permits required for operating a cleaning service in your area.

Money Needed: Starting a neighborhood cleaning service may require moderate initial investment. Budget for essential cleaning equipment such as vacuum cleaners, mops, brooms, cleaning solutions, and microfiber cloths. Allocate funds for advertising and marketing to attract clients and establish your brand. Consider obtaining liability insurance to protect your business from potential claims or damages. Set aside a budget for transportation costs and any additional cleaning supplies needed for specific client requests.

Profit Potential: The profit potential in a neighborhood cleaning service can be promising, depending on factors such as demand, competition, and the quality of your services. Cleaning services are often charged by the hour or based on the size and complexity of the cleaning task. Profit potential can be maximized by offering additional services, such as deep cleaning or organizing, and building a loyal customer base that provides repeat business and referrals.

Pros: Flexibility in setting your own schedule and availability for cleaning appointments. The potential for a steady stream of clients within your neighborhood or local community. Opportunity to offer personalized and customized cleaning services to meet individual client preferences. The satisfaction of transforming cluttered and messy spaces into clean and organized environments. The ability to establish a reputation for reliability and professionalism, leading to repeat business.

Cons: Physical demands of cleaning tasks, which may require stamina and endurance for extended periods. The need to work around the schedules and preferences of clients, including accommodating last-minute requests. The potential for encountering challenging cleaning tasks or stubborn stains that may require additional effort. The responsibility of handling cleaning supplies and equipment safely to prevent accidents or damages. The potential for negative reviews or dissatisfaction if client expectations are not met.

Do's: Set clear and transparent pricing for your cleaning services to avoid misunderstandings with clients. Provide free estimates and on-site evaluations to offer accurate quotes for cleaning projects. Use eco-friendly and safe cleaning products to cater to environmentally conscious clients. Establish strong communication channels with clients to address any concerns or special requests promptly. Offer additional services, such as deep cleaning or organizing, to increase your service offerings.

Don'ts: Avoid compromising on the quality of your cleaning services to compete on price; prioritize delivering excellent results. Don't neglect client feedback; use it to improve your services and address any areas of concern. Avoid overbooking your cleaning schedule, as it may lead to rushed or unsatisfactory work. Don't use harsh or abrasive cleaning products that may damage surfaces or harm the environment. Avoid underestimating the time and effort required for specific cleaning tasks; allocate adequate time for each project.

In conclusion, starting a neighborhood cleaning service can be a rewarding and profitable side hustle, offering the chance to provide valuable services to your local community. By understanding different cleaning techniques, using eco-friendly products, and providing reliable and efficient services, you can establish a successful cleaning business. Be mindful of the initial investment, physical demands, and client expectations associated with a cleaning service. With dedication, excellent customer service, and a commitment to quality, your neighborhood cleaning service can flourish and become a trusted and sought-after resource for homeowners and businesses in your area.

## 14. Running a lemonade stand or selling baked goods

Before embarking on a side hustle like "Running a lemonade stand or selling baked goods," it is essential to equip yourself with a comprehensive understanding of the various aspects involved to ensure a successful and enjoyable venture. In this comprehensive guide, we will explore the knowledge needed, money required to start, profit potential, pros and cons, and do's and don'ts to help you navigate the world of selling refreshing lemonade or delicious baked goods. Let's delve into the details!

Knowledge Needed: Familiarize yourself with the recipes and techniques for preparing lemonade and baked goods of high quality and taste. Acquire knowledge of food safety and hygiene practices to ensure the products you offer are safe for consumption. Understand the importance of presentation and packaging to attract customers and create a positive impression. Learn about basic accounting and record-keeping to track expenses, sales, and profits accurately. Educate yourself on local regulations and permits required for selling food items, especially if operating in public spaces.

Money Needed: Starting a lemonade stand or selling baked goods may require a modest initial investment. Budget for ingredients, equipment, and packaging materials necessary to prepare and present your products. Allocate funds for marketing and promotion to attract potential customers. Consider obtaining liability insurance to protect yourself from potential claims or incidents. Set aside a budget for any necessary permits or licenses required by local authorities for selling food items in your area.

Profit Potential: The profit potential in running a lemonade stand or selling baked goods can vary based on factors such as location, product quality, and customer demand. Earnings can be maximized by offering competitive pricing, providing excellent customer service, and seeking repeat business from satisfied customers. The profit potential may be higher during peak seasons, events, or special occasions that attract more potential customers.

Pros: Flexibility in choosing the hours and locations for your lemonade stand or baked goods sales. The opportunity to showcase your culinary skills and creativity through unique recipes and flavors. The satisfaction of providing refreshment or delight to customers through your products. The potential to build a loyal customer base through positive experiences and word-of-mouth referrals. The chance to develop valuable entrepreneurial skills, such as budgeting, marketing, and customer relations.

Cons: Seasonal demand for lemonade stands or baked goods sales may result in fluctuating income. The physical demands of food preparation and sales, especially during busy periods. The need to comply with food safety regulations and maintain high standards of cleanliness and hygiene. Potential competition from other food vendors or businesses offering similar products. The responsibility of managing inventory and waste to minimize losses and expenses.

Do's: Offer high-quality and delicious products to attract and retain customers. Use fresh and high-quality ingredients to enhance the taste and appeal of your lemonade and baked goods. Display and package your products attractively to entice customers and create a positive impression. Provide excellent customer service and engage with customers in a friendly and approachable manner. Adhere to food safety guidelines and regulations to ensure the safety of your products.

Don'ts: Avoid compromising on the quality of your products to compete on price; prioritize taste and freshness. Don't overlook the importance of cleanliness and hygiene in food preparation and sales. Avoid underestimating the demand or overestimating the quantity of products needed, leading to wastage or stockouts. Don't neglect marketing efforts; utilize social media and local advertising to attract customers. Avoid setting up your lemonade stand or selling baked goods in unauthorized or prohibited locations.

In conclusion, running a lemonade stand or selling baked goods can be a rewarding and enjoyable side hustle, offering the opportunity to showcase your culinary skills and create memorable experiences for customers. By understanding food safety regulations, offering high-quality products, and providing excellent customer service, you can establish a successful and profitable venture. Be mindful of the initial investment, seasonal demand, and food safety considerations associated with selling lemonade or baked goods. With dedication, creativity, and a commitment to customer satisfaction, your lemonade stand or baked goods sales side hustle can flourish and become a delightful addition to your community or events.

## 15. Offering carpool services for busy parents or coworkers

Before embarking on a side hustle like "Offering carpool services for busy parents or coworkers," it is crucial to equip yourself with a comprehensive understanding of the various aspects involved to ensure a successful and rewarding venture. In this comprehensive guide, we will explore the knowledge needed, money required to start, profit potential, pros and cons, and do's and don'ts to help you navigate the world of carpool services. Let's delve into the details!

Knowledge Needed: Familiarize yourself with the local traffic regulations and road safety guidelines to ensure safe and legal carpooling practices. Acquire knowledge of different routes and alternative routes to optimize travel time for your passengers. Understand effective communication and coordination to arrange pick-up and drop-off schedules with busy parents or coworkers. Educate yourself on any special needs or preferences of your passengers, such as car seat requirements or preferred drop-off points.

Money Needed: Starting a carpool service may require minimal initial investment. Budget for transportation costs, including fuel and maintenance for your vehicle. Allocate funds for car insurance, ensuring that you have adequate coverage for carpooling activities. Consider obtaining a commercial auto insurance policy to protect yourself and your passengers. Set aside a budget for marketing and promotion to attract potential clients and build a customer base.

Profit Potential: The profit potential in offering carpool services can vary based on factors such as demand, location, and the number of clients you serve. Carpool drivers typically charge a fee per ride or a weekly/monthly fee, depending on the arrangement. Profit potential can be maximized by providing reliable and punctual services, offering competitive pricing, and establishing long-term contracts with regular clients.

Pros: Flexibility in setting your own schedule and availability for carpooling activities. The opportunity to build connections and relationships with busy parents or coworkers in your community or workplace. The potential to contribute to reducing traffic congestion and environmental impact by sharing rides. The satisfaction of helping parents or coworkers save time and reduce stress by offering reliable transportation solutions. The chance to turn your regular commute into a profitable and purposeful side hustle.

Cons: The need to adhere to strict time schedules and be punctual for pick-ups and drop-offs. Potential fluctuations in demand, leading to varying income levels depending on the number of clients. The responsibility of ensuring the safety and comfort of your passengers during the carpool rides. The potential for conflicts or disagreements with clients regarding scheduling or other carpooling arrangements. The challenge of managing multiple clients with different pick-up and drop-off locations.

Do's: Maintain a reliable and punctual schedule to build trust and reliability with your carpool clients. Communicate effectively with parents or coworkers to coordinate pick-up and drop-off times and locations. Offer a clean and comfortable car environment for your passengers to enjoy during the rides. Provide safe and responsible driving practices to ensure the well-being of your passengers. Consider offering additional services, such as organizing carpool groups or providing snacks during the rides, to enhance the customer experience.

Don'ts: Avoid deviating from agreed-upon schedules or routes without prior communication and agreement from your clients. Don't compromise on the safety and comfort of your passengers by engaging in reckless driving or distracted behaviors. Avoid overbooking your carpool services, ensuring that you can provide quality service to each client. Don't forget to keep detailed records of your carpool activities and financial transactions for proper accounting and record-keeping. Avoid engaging in any form of discrimination or bias while providing carpool services to coworkers or clients.

In conclusion, offering carpool services for busy parents or coworkers can be a rewarding and purposeful side hustle, providing a valuable transportation solution for your community or workplace. By understanding road safety, maintaining a reliable schedule, and providing excellent customer service, you can establish a successful and profitable carpooling venture. Be mindful of the initial investment, car insurance, and the responsibilities associated with providing carpool services. With dedication, effective communication, and a commitment to passenger safety, your carpool service can flourish and become a trusted and sought-after resource for parents or coworkers in need of reliable transportation solutions.

## 16. Renting out camping equipment or outdoor gear

Before delving into a side hustle like "Renting out camping equipment or outdoor gear," it is essential to gain a comprehensive understanding of the various aspects involved to ensure a successful and rewarding venture. In this comprehensive guide, we will explore the knowledge needed, money required to start, profit potential, pros and cons, tips, and do's and don'ts to help you navigate the world of renting outdoor equipment. Let's delve into the details!

Knowledge Needed: Familiarize yourself with different types of camping and outdoor gear, including tents, sleeping bags, camping stoves, backpacks, and more. Acquire knowledge of the quality and durability of different equipment brands and models to ensure you offer reliable and well-maintained gear to your customers. Understand the various camping and outdoor activities that your gear can cater to, such as hiking, backpacking, or family camping. Educate yourself on proper gear maintenance and cleaning to extend the lifespan of your equipment.

Money Needed: Starting a rental service for camping equipment or outdoor gear may require a significant initial investment. Budget for purchasing a range of high-quality gear to cater to different customer preferences and needs. Allocate funds for storage and maintenance facilities to ensure the equipment remains in top condition. Consider additional costs, such as insurance for equipment and liability coverage. Set aside a marketing budget to promote your rental service and attract customers.

Profit Potential: The profit potential in renting out camping equipment and outdoor gear can be promising, especially in areas with high outdoor recreational activities. Earnings are based on the rental fees charged to customers for different gear items and rental durations. Profit potential can be maximized by providing excellent customer service, offering a diverse selection of gear, and strategically pricing your rental packages to attract both occasional and regular outdoor enthusiasts.

Pros: Flexibility in catering to a wide range of customers, from occasional campers to seasoned outdoor adventurers. The opportunity to contribute to the outdoor recreation community by providing access to quality gear. The potential to build long-term relationships with customers who return for repeated rentals. The satisfaction of facilitating memorable outdoor experiences for your customers. The chance to turn your passion for the outdoors into a profitable business.

Cons: The need to invest in a substantial initial inventory of camping equipment and gear. Potential wear and tear on the equipment, requiring regular maintenance and replacements. The responsibility of ensuring all equipment is clean, functional, and safe for customer use. The challenge of handling logistics and coordinating equipment pick-ups and drop-offs efficiently. The risk of damage or loss of gear, necessitating a robust system for managing inventory and insurance coverage.

Tips: Offer a diverse selection of camping and outdoor gear to cater to various outdoor activities and customer preferences. Consider providing package deals for customers, including essential camping items for convenience. Create a user-friendly online platform for customers to browse available gear and make reservations. Build partnerships with local outdoor organizations or event organizers to attract a broader customer base. Offer gear tutorials or informational resources to help customers make informed gear selections.

Do's: Regularly inspect and maintain your camping equipment to ensure it is in top condition for rental. Provide clear and transparent pricing and rental policies for customers. Respond promptly to customer inquiries and be attentive to their needs and preferences. Offer flexible rental durations to accommodate both short and extended outdoor trips. Develop a reservation system to manage gear availability and avoid overbooking.

Don'ts: Avoid neglecting customer feedback; use it to improve your gear selection and customer experience. Don't compromise on the quality and safety of your equipment to cut costs. Avoid overpricing your gear rentals, as it may discourage potential customers. Don't overlook the importance of marketing and promoting your rental service to attract customers.

In conclusion, renting out camping equipment or outdoor gear can be a rewarding and profitable side hustle, providing outdoor enthusiasts with access to quality gear for their adventures. By understanding outdoor gear, investing in a diverse inventory, and offering excellent customer service, you can establish a successful rental business. Be mindful of the initial investment, gear maintenance, and customer feedback. With dedication, attention to detail, and a passion for the outdoors, your camping equipment rental service can flourish and become a trusted resource for outdoor enthusiasts seeking memorable and well-equipped adventures.

## 17. Organizing garage sales for others

Before venturing into a side hustle like "Organizing garage sales for others," it is crucial to gain a comprehensive understanding of the various aspects involved to ensure a successful and profitable venture. In this comprehensive guide, we will explore the knowledge needed, money required to start, profit potential, pros and cons, tips, and do's and don'ts to help you navigate the world of garage sale organization. Let's delve into the details!

Knowledge Needed: Familiarize yourself with the process of organizing and planning garage sales, including pricing items, setting up displays, and attracting potential buyers. Acquire knowledge of the local regulations and permits required for holding garage sales in different neighborhoods or communities. Understand effective marketing and advertising strategies to promote garage sales and attract a broad customer base. Educate yourself on different pricing strategies to maximize profits while ensuring fair deals for both sellers and buyers.

Money Needed: Starting a garage sale organization service may require minimal initial investment. Budget for marketing materials, such as flyers or posters, to promote garage sales. Allocate funds for transportation costs, especially if you need to travel to clients' locations to organize their sales. Consider obtaining liability insurance to protect yourself from potential accidents or damages during garage sales. Set aside a budget for purchasing any necessary equipment, such as tables or display racks, to enhance the presentation of items.

Profit Potential: The profit potential in organizing garage sales for others can vary based on factors such as the number of clients, the success of individual sales, and the commission or fee charged for your services. Earnings are typically based on a percentage of the total sales or a fixed fee agreed upon with your clients. Profit potential can be maximized by providing exceptional organizational skills, attracting a diverse range of sellers and buyers, and offering value-added services to enhance the overall garage sale experience.

Pros: Flexibility in setting your schedule and availability for organizing garage sales. The opportunity to assist individuals in decluttering and profiting from their unwanted items. The potential to build a loyal customer base through satisfied clients who seek your services for future garage sales. The satisfaction of transforming cluttered spaces into organized and attractive sale events. The chance to turn your organizational skills into a rewarding and purposeful side hustle.

Cons: The need to coordinate with different clients, potentially resulting in varying schedules and demands. The physical demands of setting up and organizing items during garage sales, especially in outdoor settings. The challenge of managing multiple sales and ensuring that each event runs smoothly. The potential for unpredictable weather conditions that may impact outdoor garage sales. The responsibility of handling valuable items and cash during sales, requiring trustworthiness and security measures.

Tips: Offer a range of services, including pricing assistance, item categorization, and promotional materials to attract sellers. Create a user-friendly online platform for clients to book your services and access resources for organizing their sales. Establish a network of potential buyers through social media or local community groups to enhance sales traffic. Consider offering package deals for clients with multiple garage sales to incentivize repeat business. Provide guidance on setting up appealing displays and organizing items effectively to attract buyers.

Do's: Communicate clearly and professionally with clients to understand their preferences and expectations for the garage sale. Be punctual and reliable in arriving at the agreed-upon time to organize the sale. Create a detailed inventory or record of items to ensure accurate pricing and sales tracking. Offer a secure and organized payment system during the sale to streamline transactions. Follow up with clients after the sale to gather feedback and maintain a positive relationship.

Don'ts: Avoid underpricing or overpricing items without proper research or consultation with clients. Don't overlook the importance of advertising and marketing to attract a broader audience to the garage sale. Avoid making promises or commitments that you cannot fulfill during the sale organization process. Don't neglect the importance of having a contingency plan for inclement weather during outdoor garage sales. Avoid handling clients' personal belongings without their consent or supervision.

In conclusion, organizing garage sales for others can be a rewarding and profitable side hustle, offering a valuable service to individuals seeking to declutter and profit from their unwanted items. By understanding the garage sale process, providing exceptional organizational skills, and promoting sales effectively, you can establish a successful garage sale organization business. Be mindful of the initial investment, marketing efforts, and the physical demands associated with organizing multiple sales. With dedication, communication, and attention to detail, your garage sale organization service can thrive and become a trusted resource for individuals looking to streamline their decluttering process and transform their items into profitable assets.

## 18. Providing basic landscaping services

Before diving into a side hustle like "Providing basic landscaping services," it is essential to equip yourself with a comprehensive understanding of the various aspects involved to ensure a successful and rewarding venture. In this comprehensive guide, we will explore the knowledge needed, money required to start, profit potential, pros and cons, tips, and do's and don'ts to help you navigate the world of basic landscaping services. Let's delve into the details!

Knowledge Needed: Familiarize yourself with basic landscaping principles and techniques, including lawn mowing, trimming, and edging. Acquire knowledge of different plant types and their maintenance requirements to provide adequate care for gardens and green spaces. Understand proper irrigation methods and watering schedules to ensure the health and vitality of plants. Educate yourself on landscaping design principles to create visually appealing outdoor spaces for your clients.

Money Needed: Starting a basic landscaping service may require a moderate initial investment. Budget for purchasing essential landscaping tools and equipment, such as lawnmowers, trimmers, and shovels. Allocate funds for transportation costs to travel to clients' locations. Consider obtaining liability insurance to protect yourself from potential accidents or damages during landscaping work. Set aside a budget for marketing and promotion to attract potential clients and build a customer base.

Profit Potential: The profit potential in providing basic landscaping services can be promising, especially in areas with a demand for residential and commercial landscaping. Earnings are typically based on the services rendered, such as lawn mowing, gardening, and landscape design. Profit potential can be maximized by providing excellent customer service, offering a range of landscaping services, and seeking repeat business from satisfied clients.

Pros: Flexibility in setting your schedule and availability for landscaping projects. The opportunity to work outdoors and enjoy the satisfaction of transforming outdoor spaces. The potential to build long-term relationships with clients who seek your services for regular maintenance and improvements. The chance to utilize your creativity and landscaping skills to enhance the beauty of properties. The possibility to turn your passion for landscaping into a profitable and enjoyable side hustle.

Cons: The physical demands of landscaping work, especially during hot weather or challenging terrains. Potential fluctuations in demand, leading to varying income levels throughout the year. The responsibility of maintaining and repairing landscaping equipment for efficient operations. The challenge of managing multiple clients and coordinating schedules for timely service. The potential for competition from other landscaping service providers in your area.

Tips: Offer a range of landscaping services, including lawn maintenance, gardening, and landscape design, to cater to different client needs. Create a portfolio of your past landscaping projects to showcase your expertise and attract potential clients. Establish a referral program to incentivize satisfied clients to recommend your services to others. Invest in ongoing learning and training to stay updated on the latest landscaping trends and techniques. Offer seasonal promotions or discounts to attract new clients and encourage repeat business.

Do's: Communicate effectively with clients to understand their landscaping preferences and expectations. Be punctual and reliable in arriving at the agreed-upon time for landscaping services. Provide clear and transparent pricing for your landscaping services to avoid misunderstandings. Follow ethical and environmentally-friendly landscaping practices to promote sustainability. Establish a system for proper disposal of yard waste and debris after completing landscaping projects.

Don'ts: Avoid overpromising or guaranteeing results that may be beyond your expertise or control. Don't neglect the importance of safety precautions during landscaping work, especially when using power tools or equipment. Avoid neglecting regular maintenance of landscaping tools and equipment to ensure their longevity and efficiency. Don't disregard the significance of customer feedback; use it to improve your landscaping services and customer experience. Avoid performing landscaping work on properties without proper authorization or consent from the property owner.

In conclusion, providing basic landscaping services can be a rewarding and profitable side hustle, offering a valuable service to clients seeking to beautify and maintain their outdoor spaces. By understanding landscaping principles, investing in essential tools, and providing excellent customer service, you can establish a successful landscaping business. Be mindful of the initial investment, marketing efforts, and the physical demands associated with landscaping projects. With dedication, creativity, and attention to detail, your basic landscaping service can flourish and become a trusted resource for property owners seeking to enhance the aesthetics and value of their outdoor spaces.

## 19. Creating and selling digital art or designs

Before embarking on a side hustle like "Creating and selling digital art or designs," it is vital to equip yourself with a comprehensive understanding of the various aspects involved to ensure a successful and rewarding venture. In this comprehensive guide, we will explore the knowledge needed, money required to start, profit potential, pros and cons, tips, and do's and don'ts to help you navigate the world of digital art and design entrepreneurship. Let's delve into the details!

Knowledge Needed: Familiarize yourself with various digital art and design tools and software, such as Adobe Photoshop, Illustrator, or Procreate, to create high-quality and professional designs. Acquire knowledge of different art styles, trends, and techniques to cater to diverse customer preferences. Understand the principles of copyright and intellectual property rights to protect your own creations and avoid legal issues. Educate yourself on effective digital marketing strategies to promote your artwork and reach a broader audience.

Money Needed: Starting a digital art and design side hustle may require a moderate initial investment. Budget for purchasing or subscribing to essential digital art software and tools. Allocate funds for advertising and marketing to build brand awareness and attract potential customers.

Consider investing in professional-grade equipment, such as a high-resolution monitor or graphic tablet, to enhance the quality of your artwork. Set aside a budget for web hosting or online marketplaces to showcase and sell your digital designs.

Profit Potential: The profit potential in creating and selling digital art or designs can be promising, especially in the era of online marketplaces and digital content demand. Earnings are typically based on the sales of your digital designs through various channels, such as online platforms or custom commissions. Profit potential can be maximized by continuously creating new and engaging designs, building a loyal customer base, and leveraging social media and digital marketing to expand your reach.

Pros: Flexibility in managing your schedule and working from the comfort of your own space. The opportunity to express your creativity and showcase your artistic talent to the world. The potential to generate passive income through the sale of digital downloads and licensing of your artwork. The chance to connect with a global audience and receive feedback and appreciation for your designs. The possibility to turn your passion for art into a profitable and fulfilling side hustle.

Cons: The competitive nature of the digital art market, requiring consistent innovation and uniqueness to stand out. Potential challenges in attracting customers and building a reputation in the crowded digital art space. The responsibility of handling customer inquiries, providing support, and delivering digital files efficiently. The risk of copyright infringement or unauthorized use of your artwork, necessitating vigilant monitoring and protection. The potential for fluctuations in income based on market trends and demand for specific design styles.

Tips: Offer a diverse range of digital art and design products to cater to different niches and customer preferences. Create a compelling and visually appealing online portfolio or shop to showcase your artwork professionally. Establish a recognizable brand identity and signature style to make your designs easily identifiable. Collaborate with other artists or influencers to expand your reach and attract new customers. Stay up-to-date with the latest design trends and adapt your creations to suit current market demands.

Do's: Protect your artwork and designs by adding watermarks or copyright notices to your digital files. Respect copyright and intellectual property rights by using only licensed or royalty-free resources in your creations. Offer transparent and fair pricing for your digital art downloads and custom commissions. Engage with your audience through social media or a blog to build a loyal following and connect with potential customers. Regularly update your portfolio or online shop with fresh designs to keep your offerings relevant and exciting.

Don'ts: Avoid using copyrighted material or designs owned by others without proper authorization or licensing. Don't compromise on the quality of your artwork; aim for excellence in every creation. Avoid neglecting customer inquiries or feedback; prioritize prompt and courteous communication. Don't undersell your artwork or undervalue your talent; price your designs competitively and fairly. Avoid spammy or aggressive marketing tactics; instead, focus on building organic and meaningful connections with your audience.

In conclusion, creating and selling digital art or designs can be a fulfilling and profitable side hustle, allowing you to showcase your artistic talent and reach a global audience. By understanding digital art tools, investing in quality equipment, and implementing effective marketing strategies, you can establish a successful digital art and design business. Be mindful of the initial investment, copyright protection, and customer engagement. With dedication, creativity, and a passion for art, your digital art side hustle can flourish and become a sought-after source of beautiful and inspiring creations.

## Thea Stewart
### Member of PageTitans

I wanted to remind you of the **free gift** that you are welcome to download. There is free additional content.

To download your free copy, simply follow the link or scan the QR code. Please **don't forget to subscribe** to stay in touch with PageTitans.

**http://pagetitans.com?page=000I5e**

## 20. Providing graphic design services

Before embarking on a side hustle like "Providing graphic design services," it is essential to equip yourself with a comprehensive understanding of the various aspects involved to ensure a successful and rewarding venture. In this comprehensive guide, we will explore the knowledge needed, money required to start, profit potential, pros and cons, tips, and do's and don'ts to help you navigate the world of graphic design entrepreneurship. Let's delve into the details!

Knowledge Needed: Familiarize yourself with graphic design principles and techniques, including layout, color theory, typography, and composition. Acquire proficiency in graphic design software, such as Adobe Illustrator, Photoshop, or InDesign, to create professional and high-quality designs. Understand various design styles and trends to cater to diverse client preferences and industries. Educate yourself on copyright laws and intellectual property rights to protect your own creations and respect others' work. Familiarize yourself with effective communication and client management skills to understand clients' needs and deliver exceptional results.

Money Needed: Starting a graphic design service side hustle may require a moderate initial investment. Budget for purchasing or subscribing to essential graphic design software and tools. Allocate funds for marketing and promotion to build brand awareness and attract potential clients. Consider investing in a professional-grade computer or graphic tablet to enhance the quality and efficiency of your design work. Set aside a budget for web hosting or portfolio platforms to showcase your work and attract potential clients.

Profit Potential: The profit potential in providing graphic design services can be promising, especially with the increasing demand for design work across various industries. Earnings are typically based on project fees or hourly rates charged to clients for design services. Profit potential can be maximized by delivering high-quality designs, building a strong portfolio, establishing a loyal client base, and offering additional services such as branding or social media design.

Pros: Flexibility in managing your schedule and working from any location with an internet connection. The opportunity to express your creativity and artistic talent through various design projects. The potential to work with diverse clients from different industries and create impactful designs. The chance to build a professional reputation and grow your graphic design skills through real-world projects. The possibility to turn your passion for design into a profitable and fulfilling side hustle.

Cons: The competitive nature of the graphic design market, requiring constant innovation and continuous learning to stay relevant. Potential challenges in attracting clients initially, especially when starting with limited experience or a small portfolio. The responsibility of managing multiple projects and meeting deadlines for different clients simultaneously. The potential for subjective feedback from clients, requiring open communication and the ability to handle constructive criticism. The risk of burnout due to the demanding nature of graphic design work and managing client expectations.

Tips: Build a diverse portfolio showcasing various design styles and projects to attract a wide range of clients. Establish a professional website or portfolio platform to showcase your work and provide a seamless way for potential clients to contact you. Network with other professionals in related industries to gain referrals and expand your client base. Offer a range of graphic design services, such as logo design, marketing materials, and social media graphics, to cater to different client needs. Provide exceptional customer service, including clear communication and regular project updates, to build trust with clients and encourage repeat business.

Do's: Respect copyright laws and intellectual property rights by using licensed or royalty-free resources in your designs. Set clear project timelines and deliverables with clients to manage expectations and avoid misunderstandings. Regularly update your graphic design skills through online tutorials, courses, or workshops to stay ahead in the industry. Use social media and online platforms to showcase your work and connect with potential clients. Establish a straightforward and transparent pricing structure for your graphic design services to avoid confusion.

Don'ts: Avoid using copyrighted material or designs owned by others without proper authorization or licensing. Don't overpromise or guarantee results that may be beyond your control or expertise. Avoid taking on more projects than you can handle to maintain the quality of your work and meet client deadlines. Don't undervalue your design skills or undercharge for your services; price your work competitively based on your expertise and market demand. Avoid neglecting client feedback or requests; prioritize open communication and address any concerns promptly.

In conclusion, providing graphic design services can be a fulfilling and profitable side hustle, allowing you to express your creativity and work with diverse clients. By understanding design principles, investing in quality tools, and offering excellent customer service, you can establish a successful graphic design business. Be mindful of the initial investment, continuous learning, and managing client expectations. With dedication, creativity, and a passion for design, your graphic design side hustle can thrive and become a trusted source for visually captivating and impactful designs.

## 21. Freelance writing or content creation

Before venturing into a side hustle like "Freelance writing or content creation," it is essential to equip yourself with a comprehensive understanding of the various aspects involved to ensure a successful and rewarding venture. In this comprehensive guide, we will explore the knowledge needed, money required to start, profit potential, pros and cons, tips, and do's and don'ts to help you navigate the world of freelance writing and content creation entrepreneurship. Let's delve into the details!

Knowledge Needed: Familiarize yourself with different writing styles, including creative writing, copywriting, blog writing, and technical writing, to cater to diverse client needs. Acquire proficiency in grammar, punctuation, and language usage to deliver error-free and professional content. Understand various content creation platforms and digital marketing trends to create content that resonates with target audiences. Educate yourself on SEO principles and keyword optimization to enhance the visibility and reach of your content. Familiarize yourself with industry-specific knowledge to write well-informed and authoritative pieces.

Money Needed: Starting a freelance writing or content creation side hustle may require a minimal initial investment. Budget for a reliable computer or laptop, high-speed internet, and necessary writing tools. Allocate funds for online portfolio creation or website hosting to showcase your writing samples and attract potential clients. Consider investing in writing courses or workshops to improve your skills and expand your knowledge. Set aside a budget for marketing and promotion to reach potential clients and build a strong online presence.

Profit Potential: The profit potential in freelance writing and content creation can be promising, especially with the growing demand for digital content across industries. Earnings are typically based on the type and complexity of writing projects, word count, and client agreements. Profit potential can be maximized by offering specialized writing services, building a diverse client base, and delivering high-quality and engaging content.

Pros: Flexibility in managing your schedule and working from any location with internet access. The opportunity to express your creativity and passion for writing through various projects. The potential to work with clients from diverse industries and gain insights into different topics. The chance to build a strong online presence and expand your reach through social media and content platforms. The possibility to turn your love for writing into a profitable and fulfilling side hustle.

Cons: The competitive nature of the freelance writing market, requiring continuous effort to stand out and secure clients. Potential challenges in finding consistent work initially, especially when building your portfolio and reputation. The responsibility of managing multiple projects and meeting deadlines for various clients simultaneously. The potential for subjective feedback from clients, requiring adaptability and open communication. The risk of experiencing burnout due to the demanding nature of writing projects and managing client expectations.

Tips: Create a diverse writing portfolio showcasing different writing styles and topics to attract a wide range of clients. Establish a professional website or blog to showcase your writing skills and create a professional online presence. Network with other writers and professionals in related industries to gain referrals and build connections. Offer a range of writing services, such as blog posts, articles, website content, and social media posts, to cater to diverse client needs. Provide exceptional customer service, including clear communication and prompt responses, to build trust with clients.

Do's: Respect deadlines and deliver high-quality content to build a reputation for reliability and professionalism. Use writing tools and software to enhance your writing efficiency and accuracy. Regularly update your writing skills through reading, workshops, and online courses to stay relevant in the industry. Utilize social media platforms and content marketing strategies to reach potential clients and promote your writing services. Be transparent and professional in your pricing and contract terms with clients.

Don'ts: Avoid using copyrighted material or plagiarizing content from other sources in your writing. Don't overcommit to projects beyond your capacity, risking the quality of your work and meeting deadlines. Avoid underselling your writing skills or undercharging for your services; price your work competitively based on your expertise and market demand. Don't neglect the importance of regular self-promotion and marketing to attract new clients and grow your freelance writing business. Avoid neglecting client feedback or requests; prioritize open communication and address any concerns promptly.

In conclusion, freelance writing and content creation can be a rewarding and profitable side hustle, allowing you to express your creativity and writing talent while serving diverse clients. By understanding writing principles, investing in essential tools, and offering exceptional customer service, you can establish a successful freelance writing business. Be mindful of continuous learning, managing client expectations, and staying competitive in the writing market. With dedication, creativity, and a passion for writing, your freelance writing side hustle can thrive and become a trusted resource for impactful and engaging content.

## 22. Online tutoring or teaching

Before delving into a side hustle like "Online tutoring or teaching," it's essential to equip yourself with a comprehensive understanding of the various aspects involved to ensure a successful and rewarding venture. In this comprehensive guide, we will explore the knowledge needed, money required to start, profit potential, pros and cons, tips, and do's and don'ts to help you navigate the world of online tutoring and teaching entrepreneurship. Let's delve into the details!

Knowledge Needed: Possess in-depth knowledge and expertise in the subject or subjects you plan to tutor or teach online. Understand various online teaching platforms and tools, such as video conferencing software and virtual whiteboards, to conduct effective virtual lessons. Familiarize yourself with different teaching methods and strategies to cater to diverse learning styles. Educate yourself on effective communication and engagement techniques to keep students motivated and actively participating in online lessons. Stay updated with the latest educational trends and technologies to enhance the quality of your online teaching.

Money Needed: Starting an online tutoring or teaching side hustle may require a minimal initial investment. Budget for a reliable computer or laptop, high-quality webcam, and a stable internet connection to facilitate seamless online interactions. Allocate funds for relevant teaching materials, such as textbooks or online resources, to supplement your lessons. Consider investing in additional teaching certifications or training to enhance your credibility and attract more students. Set aside a budget for marketing and promotion to reach potential students and build your online teaching presence.

Profit Potential: The profit potential in online tutoring and teaching can be promising, especially with the increasing demand for remote education and personalized learning. Earnings are typically based on the number of students, lesson fees, and the subject or level of expertise offered. Profit potential can be maximized by offering specialized tutoring services, building a strong reputation, and attracting a steady stream of students.

Pros: Flexibility in managing your schedule and the ability to reach students from different geographic locations. The opportunity to make a positive impact on students' learning and academic success. The potential to teach a variety of subjects or topics, catering to your expertise and interests. The chance to leverage technology and multimedia to enhance the learning experience. The possibility to turn your passion for education into a profitable and fulfilling side hustle.

Cons: The competitive nature of the online tutoring and teaching market, requiring continuous efforts to attract and retain students. Potential challenges in establishing credibility and building trust as an online educator, especially in a saturated market. The responsibility of adapting teaching techniques to suit virtual learning environments and individual student needs. The potential for technical issues during online lessons, necessitating troubleshooting and backup plans. The risk of variable income based on student demand and seasonal fluctuations.

Tips: Identify your target audience and the subjects or areas where you have expertise to narrow down your online tutoring focus. Create a professional and inviting online presence, such as a website or profile on tutoring platforms, to showcase your credentials and attract students. Offer a free trial or consultation to prospective students to demonstrate your teaching style and build trust. Provide personalized and tailored learning plans to meet individual student needs and learning goals. Utilize interactive tools and multimedia to enhance student engagement and understanding during online lessons.

Do's: Set clear expectations and communication guidelines with students to establish a positive learning environment. Stay organized with lesson planning and materials to ensure smooth online teaching sessions. Encourage active participation and feedback from students to enhance their learning experience. Emphasize regular practice and review to reinforce learning concepts and improve student retention.

Be adaptable and patient with technology and learning challenges that students may face during online lessons.

Don'ts: Avoid overcommitting to a high number of students if it compromises the quality of your teaching. Don't neglect ongoing professional development to stay updated with the latest teaching strategies and technology. Avoid using complex technical terms or jargon during online lessons; use simple and clear language to facilitate student understanding. Don't compare your rates solely based on competitors; consider your expertise, teaching style, and the value you provide to students. Avoid overloading students with excessive assignments or tasks that may lead to burnout or disengagement.

In conclusion, online tutoring and teaching can be a rewarding and profitable side hustle, offering the flexibility to share your knowledge and passion for education with students worldwide. By possessing subject expertise, investing in necessary tools, and utilizing effective teaching methods, you can establish a successful online tutoring business. Be mindful of continuous learning, student engagement, and building a strong online presence. With dedication, adaptability, and a commitment to student success, your online tutoring side hustle can flourish and become a trusted resource for empowering and enriching students' learning journeys.

## 23. Selling print-on-demand products (e.g., t-shirts, books, mugs)

Before diving into a side hustle like "Selling print-on-demand products (e.g., t-shirts, books, mugs, tote bags)," it's essential to equip yourself with a comprehensive understanding of the various aspects involved to ensure a successful and rewarding venture. In this comprehensive guide, we will explore the knowledge needed, money required to start, profit potential, pros and cons, tips, and do's and don'ts to help you navigate the world of print-on-demand entrepreneurship. Let's delve into the details!

Knowledge Needed: Familiarize yourself with the print-on-demand business model and how it operates, including the process of creating, designing, and selling custom products. Understand various print-on-demand platforms and their features, such as integration with e-commerce websites and fulfillment services. Educate yourself on copyright laws and intellectual property rights to ensure that your designs comply with legal requirements. Acquire basic graphic design skills or collaborate with designers to create appealing and marketable designs for your products. Stay updated with current design trends and popular niches to cater to diverse customer preferences.

Money Needed: Starting a print-on-demand side hustle may require a moderate initial investment, depending on your product range and marketing strategies. Budget for a reliable computer or laptop to manage your online store and design creation. Allocate funds for graphic design software and design assets to create professional-quality product designs.

Consider investing in marketing and advertising to promote your products and attract customers. Set aside a budget for sample products to evaluate the quality and design before offering them for sale.

Profit Potential: The profit potential in the print-on-demand business can be promising, given the low upfront costs and the ability to sell a wide range of custom products to a global audience. Earnings are typically based on the difference between the product's selling price and the production and fulfillment costs. Profit potential can be maximized by offering unique and trending designs, optimizing product listings for better visibility, and exploring various marketing channels to reach a broader customer base.

Pros: Low upfront costs and minimal inventory management, as products are only printed and shipped upon customer orders. The opportunity to express creativity and showcase artistic talents through custom designs. The potential to reach a global audience through print-on-demand platforms and e-commerce websites. The chance to offer a diverse product range, catering to various niches and customer interests. The possibility to turn your passion for design and entrepreneurship into a profitable and fulfilling side hustle.

Cons: The competitive nature of the print-on-demand market, requiring innovative and eye-catching designs to stand out. Potential challenges in promoting and marketing your products effectively to attract customers. The responsibility of managing customer inquiries, returns, and shipping-related issues. The potential for limited profit margins, especially with intense competition in popular product categories. The risk of copyright infringement or design similarities with other sellers, leading to legal complications.

Tips: Identify a niche or target market for your print-on-demand products to tailor your designs and marketing efforts accordingly. Create a strong brand identity and cohesive product line to build a recognizable and memorable brand. Offer a variety of product options, such as t-shirts, hoodies, mugs, and notebooks, to appeal to different customer preferences. Utilize social media and influencer marketing to showcase your products and reach potential customers. Use high-quality product images and clear product descriptions to enhance customer confidence and conversion rates.

Do's: Regularly update your product offerings with fresh designs and seasonal themes to keep customers engaged. Collaborate with influencers or brand ambassadors to promote your print-on-demand products to their followers. Utilize search engine optimization (SEO) techniques to improve the visibility of your product listings on print-on-demand platforms and search engines. Utilize customer feedback and reviews to improve your product offerings and customer experience. Offer excellent customer service to build trust and loyalty with your customers.

Don'ts: Avoid using copyrighted or trademarked designs without proper authorization or licensing. Don't overprice your products, as competitive pricing can attract more customers and increase sales. Avoid relying solely on one print-on-demand platform; consider diversifying your sales channels to reach a broader audience. Don't compromise on the quality of your products or shipping services, as customer satisfaction is crucial for long-term success. Avoid copying or imitating other sellers' designs; focus on creating original and unique designs that reflect your brand.

In conclusion, selling print-on-demand products can be a rewarding and profitable side hustle, offering creative freedom and a global reach. By understanding the print-on-demand business model, investing in quality design assets, and marketing your products effectively, you can establish a successful print-on-demand business. Be mindful of continuous learning, customer feedback, and staying ahead of design trends. With dedication, innovation, and a passion for design, your print-on-demand side hustle can flourish and become a go-to destination for custom and trendy products.

## 24. Dropshipping products through an e-commerce store

Before delving into a side hustle like "Dropshipping products through an e-commerce store," it's essential to equip yourself with a comprehensive understanding of the various aspects involved to ensure a successful and rewarding venture. In this comprehensive guide, we will explore the knowledge needed, money required to start, profit potential, pros and cons, tips, and do's and don'ts to help you navigate the world of dropshipping entrepreneurship. Let's delve into the details!

Knowledge Needed: Familiarize yourself with the dropshipping business model and how it operates, including the role of suppliers, inventory management, and order fulfillment. Understand various e-commerce platforms and how to set up and manage an online store effectively. Educate yourself on product sourcing, supplier selection, and negotiation to ensure a reliable and efficient supply chain. Acquire marketing and branding knowledge to promote and differentiate your dropshipping store in a competitive market. Stay updated with industry trends and customer preferences to curate a diverse and appealing product selection.

Money Needed: Starting a dropshipping side hustle may require a moderate initial investment, depending on your chosen niche and marketing strategies. Budget for e-commerce platform fees, website hosting, and domain registration to establish your online store. Allocate funds for marketing and advertising to attract potential customers to your store. Consider investing in professional product images and content to enhance the visual appeal and credibility of your store. Set aside a budget for customer support and order tracking to ensure a smooth and positive shopping experience for your customers.

Profit Potential: The profit potential in dropshipping can be promising, given the low upfront costs and the ability to offer a wide range of products without holding physical inventory. Earnings are typically based on the difference between the product's selling price and the wholesale price charged by the supplier. Profit potential can be maximized by selecting products with attractive profit margins, optimizing product listings for better visibility, and implementing effective marketing strategies to drive sales.

Pros: Low upfront investment and inventory costs, as products are sourced from suppliers only upon customer orders. The flexibility to manage and operate your dropshipping store from anywhere with an internet connection. The potential to offer a diverse product range and quickly adapt to market trends and customer demands. The chance to build and grow your e-commerce brand, leading to potential long-term success. The possibility to turn your passion for entrepreneurship into a profitable and scalable side hustle.

Cons: The reliance on suppliers for product inventory and order fulfillment, with the risk of delays or stockouts affecting customer satisfaction. Potential challenges in finding reliable and trustworthy suppliers to maintain product quality and timely deliveries. The responsibility of handling customer inquiries, returns, and refund requests, which can be time-consuming. The potential for intense competition in popular dropshipping niches, requiring unique positioning and marketing strategies. The risk of lower profit margins, especially in highly competitive markets.

Tips: Focus on finding a niche or product category that aligns with your interests, expertise, and target audience. Build a user-friendly and visually appealing e-commerce store with clear product descriptions and high-quality images. Utilize search engine optimization (SEO) techniques to improve the visibility of your store in search engines and attract organic traffic. Offer excellent customer service, including prompt responses to inquiries and efficient order tracking. Establish transparent communication with suppliers to ensure smooth order processing and fulfillment.

Do's: Test and evaluate different product categories to identify high-demand and profitable items for your dropshipping store. Utilize social media and content marketing to create brand awareness and engage with potential customers. Monitor and analyze sales data and customer feedback to identify areas for improvement and growth. Optimize your product listings and e-commerce store for mobile devices to cater to mobile shoppers. Implement email marketing and retargeting strategies to nurture leads and encourage repeat purchases.

Don'ts: Avoid relying solely on one supplier; diversify your supplier network to mitigate potential risks. Don't overprice products, as competitive pricing can attract more customers and increase sales. Avoid using copyrighted images or content without proper authorization; prioritize legal compliance. Don't neglect customer support and timely responses to inquiries, as it can impact customer loyalty and retention. Avoid overselling or overpromising product features to prevent potential disappointments.

In conclusion, dropshipping through an e-commerce store can be a rewarding and profitable side hustle, offering flexibility and potential for scalability. By understanding the dropshipping business model, investing in a well-designed online store, and offering exceptional customer service, you can establish a successful dropshipping business. Be mindful of supplier selection, marketing efforts, and continuous monitoring of sales data to optimize your store's performance. With dedication, strategic planning, and a commitment to customer satisfaction, your dropshipping side hustle can thrive and become a valuable asset in your entrepreneurial journey.

## 25. Photography services for events or stock photos

Before embarking on a side hustle in photography services for events or stock photos, it's crucial to equip yourself with comprehensive knowledge, financial planning, and understanding the profit potential in this creative endeavor. In this comprehensive guide, we will explore the necessary knowledge, financial considerations, profit potential, pros and cons, and essential tips, do's, and don'ts to help you establish a successful photography side hustle. Let's delve into the details!

Knowledge Needed: Familiarize yourself with photography techniques, including camera settings, composition, lighting, and post-processing. Gain experience in capturing various types of events, such as weddings, parties, corporate gatherings, and family occasions. Understand the importance of storytelling through images and the ability to capture candid moments that evoke emotions. Acquire knowledge of copyright laws and model release agreements, especially when dealing with clients or stock photo submissions. Stay updated with the latest photography trends and styles to offer fresh and relevant work to your clients or stock photo agencies.

Money Needed: Starting a photography side hustle may require a moderate initial investment, depending on your current gear and the scope of services you plan to offer. Budget for a quality camera body, lenses, and essential accessories to ensure professional-grade results. Invest in a reliable computer or laptop for photo editing and managing your photography business. Allocate funds for marketing and advertising to promote your photography services or stock photos. Consider investing in photography courses or workshops to enhance your skills and knowledge.

Profit Potential: The profit potential in photography services can be promising, especially if you establish a strong client base and offer high-quality images. Earnings can vary depending on the type and scale of events you cover or the success of your stock photos. Offering both event photography and stock photos can diversify your income streams. Profit potential can be maximized by targeting specific niches or industries where demand for photography services or stock images is high.

Pros: The opportunity to pursue your passion for photography and turn it into a profitable side hustle. The flexibility to choose your working hours and availability for photography gigs or stock photo submissions. The potential to capture memorable moments for clients during events and create artistic stock photos that resonate with a broader audience. The ability to build a strong photography portfolio and gain recognition for your work. The chance to grow your photography side hustle into a full-time profession, if desired.

Cons: The initial investment in photography equipment can be significant, especially for high-quality camera bodies and lenses. The competitive nature of the photography industry, requiring continuous efforts to stand out and attract clients or stock photo buyers. The responsibility of managing client expectations, delivering high-quality images, and meeting project deadlines. The challenges of marketing and promoting your photography services or stock photos to reach a larger audience. The need to continually improve your photography skills and adapt to changing trends and technology.

Tips: Identify your photography niche or focus, such as wedding photography, corporate events, lifestyle photography, or stock photos in specific categories. Create a professional photography website or portfolio to showcase your best work and attract potential clients or stock photo buyers. Utilize social media platforms and online photography communities to network with potential clients or other photographers. Collaborate with event planners, businesses, or influencers to expand your photography client base and reach. Participate in photography contests and submissions to gain exposure and recognition for your work.

Do's: Invest in high-quality photography gear and software for capturing and editing images. Offer excellent customer service and communication to build trust and rapport with clients or stock photo buyers. Continuously improve your photography skills through workshops, tutorials, and practice. Build a diverse and appealing photography portfolio that showcases your versatility and style. Stay organized and maintain a calendar to manage photography bookings, events, or stock photo submissions effectively.

Don'ts: Don't compromise on the quality of your images, as high-quality work is crucial for client satisfaction and stock photo acceptance. Avoid over-editing or altering images beyond their natural aesthetics, as authenticity is valued in photography. Don't neglect marketing and promotion; consistently promote your photography services or stock photos to gain visibility and attract opportunities. Avoid infringing on copyright laws or using images without proper licensing or permission. Don't underestimate the value of networking and building relationships with potential clients, stock agencies, or fellow photographers.

In conclusion, photography services for events or stock photos can be a rewarding and creative side hustle, offering opportunities for self-expression and financial growth. By understanding photography techniques, investing in quality gear, and effectively marketing your services or stock photos, you can establish a successful photography side hustle. Be proactive in building your portfolio, reaching out to potential clients, and continuously honing your skills to thrive in the competitive photography industry. With passion, dedication, and a commitment to delivering exceptional images, your photography side hustle can flourish and become a valuable asset in your entrepreneurial journey.

## 26. Carrying out affiliate marketing

Before diving into the world of affiliate marketing as a side hustle, it's essential to equip yourself with the necessary knowledge, financial considerations, and an understanding of the profit potential in this digital marketing endeavor. In this comprehensive guide, we will explore the expertise needed, financial aspects, profit potential, pros and cons, and crucial tips, do's, and don'ts to help you embark on a successful affiliate marketing side hustle. Let's delve into the details!

Knowledge Needed: Familiarize yourself with the fundamentals of digital marketing, including SEO, content creation, social media marketing, and email marketing. Understand the concept of affiliate marketing, the role of affiliates, merchants, and customers, and how affiliate programs operate. Acquire knowledge of different affiliate networks and platforms, understanding their terms, conditions, and commission structures. Stay updated with industry trends, emerging affiliate marketing strategies, and new product launches to optimize your promotional efforts effectively.

Money Needed: Starting an affiliate marketing side hustle can be relatively cost-effective, but it may require some initial investment. Budget for a reliable internet connection, a website or blog for content promotion, and domain registration. Allocate funds for online advertising, social media promotions, and email marketing campaigns to drive traffic to your affiliate links. Consider investing in affiliate marketing training or courses to enhance your skills and understand the best practices in this field.

Profit Potential: The profit potential in affiliate marketing can be promising, especially if you build a strong online presence and attract a substantial audience. Earnings are typically based on commissions earned from successful referrals or sales generated through your affiliate links. Profit potential can be maximized by choosing high-converting products or services, leveraging multiple affiliate programs, and consistently optimizing your marketing strategies.

Pros: The flexibility to work from anywhere with an internet connection, allowing you to manage your affiliate marketing side hustle on your terms. The potential to earn passive income by promoting products or services that align with your target audience's interests. The opportunity to diversify income streams by promoting products across various niches and industries. The chance to leverage your existing online presence, such as a blog or social media following, to drive traffic to your affiliate links. The ability to scale your affiliate marketing efforts and potentially turn it into a full-time venture.

Cons: The need for consistent and strategic marketing efforts to attract traffic and generate affiliate sales, which can require time and effort. The challenge of standing out in a saturated affiliate marketing landscape, necessitating unique and value-driven content. The risk of depending solely on the performance of the merchant's website or product quality, which can impact affiliate earnings. The potential for conflicts of interest if promoting multiple products or services that do not align with your audience's needs or values. The necessity to comply with affiliate program rules and avoid unethical marketing practices.

Tips: Choose a niche or topic that aligns with your interests and expertise, making it easier to create valuable and engaging content. Focus on building trust and credibility with your audience by providing genuine product recommendations and honest reviews. Use data analytics and tracking tools to measure the performance of your affiliate marketing campaigns and optimize accordingly. Leverage email marketing to nurture leads, build relationships, and drive sales through personalized promotions. Collaborate with merchants or other affiliates to exchange ideas, share experiences, and enhance your affiliate marketing strategies.

Do's: Research and select reputable affiliate programs and products that resonate with your target audience. Develop a content strategy that includes blog posts, reviews, guides, and social media posts to promote affiliate products. Implement SEO best practices to improve the visibility of your affiliate content in search engine results. Focus on building a loyal and engaged audience by consistently delivering valuable and relevant content. Disclose your affiliate relationships transparently to maintain trust with your audience and comply with legal regulations.

Don'ts: Avoid promoting products or services solely based on high commission rates without considering their relevance and value to your audience. Don't engage in spammy or unethical marketing practices, such as sending unsolicited emails or using misleading advertising. Avoid overloading your audience with excessive affiliate links, as it can lead to decreased trust and engagement. Don't ignore the importance of tracking and analyzing affiliate performance to make data-driven decisions. Avoid promoting products or services that conflict with your audience's needs, interests, or values.

In conclusion, affiliate marketing offers a flexible and potentially lucrative side hustle, provided you approach it with the right knowledge, strategies, and ethical considerations. By understanding digital marketing principles, selecting the right affiliate programs, and consistently delivering valuable content, you can establish a successful affiliate marketing side hustle. Be patient, persistent, and open to learning and adapting your marketing efforts to maximize the profit potential. With dedication and a customer-centric approach, your affiliate marketing side hustle can thrive, offering you the opportunity for passive income and a rewarding entrepreneurial journey.

## 27. Starting a blog or YouTube channel and monetize through ads

Before venturing into the world of blogging or creating a YouTube channel with the intention of monetizing through ads, it is crucial to equip yourself with the necessary knowledge, financial considerations, and an understanding of the profit potential in this digital content creation endeavor. In this comprehensive guide, we will explore the expertise needed, financial aspects, profit potential, pros and cons, and essential tips, do's, and don'ts to help you embark on a successful blogging or YouTube side hustle. Let's delve into the details!

Knowledge Needed: Familiarize yourself with the fundamentals of content creation, including writing, video production, editing, and storytelling. Understand the mechanics of blogging platforms, website hosting, or YouTube channels, and how to optimize them for search engines and user engagement. Acquire knowledge of niche selection, audience targeting, and competitor analysis to create valuable and relevant content. Stay updated with industry trends, algorithm changes, and best practices in content monetization through ads.

Money Needed: Starting a blog or YouTube channel can be relatively affordable, but some initial investment may be required. Budget for domain registration, website hosting, or video equipment and editing software. Allocate funds for marketing and promotion to attract an initial audience to your blog or YouTube channel. Consider investing in online courses or workshops to enhance your content creation and marketing skills.

Profit Potential: The profit potential in blogging or YouTube monetization can be promising, but it requires dedication and consistency in content creation and audience engagement. Earnings typically come from ad revenue generated through platforms like Google AdSense. Profit potential can be maximized by producing high-quality, engaging content that attracts a substantial audience and drives significant ad impressions and clicks.

Pros: The opportunity to pursue your passion for content creation, sharing your knowledge, skills, and creativity with a global audience. The flexibility to work on your terms and create content that aligns with your interests and expertise. The potential to earn passive income through ad monetization, allowing you to generate revenue even when you're not actively creating new content. The chance to build a community of like-minded individuals who follow and engage with your blog or YouTube channel. The ability to leverage your content and audience to explore other revenue streams, such as sponsored content or merchandise sales.

Cons: The challenge of building an initial audience and gaining traction in a competitive online content landscape. The need for consistent content creation and engagement to retain and grow your audience. The potential fluctuations in ad revenue due to changes in algorithms or audience behavior. The responsibility of maintaining a consistent content schedule and managing comments and feedback from your audience. The potential time and effort required before significant ad revenue is generated.

Tips: Choose a niche or topic that you are passionate about and can sustainably create content for in the long run. Define your target audience and tailor your content to address their interests and needs. Use keyword research and SEO techniques to optimize your blog posts or YouTube videos for better visibility in search engines. Interact with your audience, respond to comments, and consider their feedback to improve your content. Collaborate with other bloggers or YouTubers to expand your reach and tap into new audiences.

Do's: Invest in quality content creation tools, such as cameras, microphones, or editing software, to produce professional-grade content. Be consistent in your content schedule to build trust and loyalty with your audience. Focus on creating valuable and engaging content that provides real value to your viewers or readers. Implement call-to-action elements in your content to encourage audience engagement and interaction. Promote your blog or YouTube channel through social media and other online platforms to attract a wider audience.

Don'ts: Avoid clickbait or misleading titles and thumbnails that may attract views but lead to disengagement. Don't compromise on content quality for the sake of quantity; focus on producing meaningful content. Avoid infringing on copyright laws or using copyrighted material without proper permission. Don't solely rely on ad revenue as your only income stream; explore other opportunities like affiliate marketing or sponsored content.

In conclusion, starting a blog or YouTube channel with the aim of monetizing through ads can be a fulfilling and potentially profitable side hustle. By honing your content creation skills, understanding your audience, and remaining consistent in your efforts, you can establish a successful platform and generate ad revenue. Embrace the challenges and be open to learning and adapting your content strategy to optimize your profit potential. With creativity, dedication, and an audience-centric approach, your blogging or YouTube side hustle can thrive, offering you the opportunity for passive income and a rewarding digital content creation journey.

## 28. Creating and selling digital products (e-books, templates)

Before embarking on a side hustle involving the creation and sale of digital products such as e-books, templates, and presets, it's essential to equip yourself with the necessary knowledge, financial considerations, and an understanding of the profit potential in the digital product market. In this comprehensive guide, we will explore the expertise needed, financial aspects, profit potential, pros and cons, and essential tips, do's, and don'ts to help you establish a successful venture in creating and selling digital products. Let's delve into the details!

Knowledge Needed: Familiarize yourself with the digital product market, identifying popular niches and target audiences for e-books, templates, and presets. Acquire expertise in content creation, design, and software tools to produce high-quality digital products. Understand copyright laws and licensing to protect your intellectual property and avoid potential legal issues. Stay updated with industry trends, customer preferences, and technological advancements to offer innovative and relevant digital products.

Money Needed: Starting a digital product side hustle can be relatively cost-effective, but some initial investment may be required. Budget for software subscriptions, design tools, or content creation resources. Allocate funds for marketing and promotion to reach your target audience effectively. Consider investing in online courses or workshops to enhance your skills in digital product creation and marketing.

Profit Potential: The profit potential in creating and selling digital products can be lucrative, provided you cater to a specific target audience and offer valuable and unique products. Earnings are typically based on the number of product sales. Profit potential can be maximized by offering a diverse range of products, establishing a strong online presence, and leveraging marketing strategies to reach a broader audience.

Pros: The opportunity to showcase your creativity and expertise through digital products that resonate with your audience. The potential for passive income, as digital products can be sold repeatedly without the need for physical inventory. The ability to reach a global audience, regardless of geographical constraints, through online platforms and marketplaces. The chance to build a loyal customer base that follows and supports your digital product offerings. The versatility to explore various digital product types and adapt your offerings based on market demand.

Cons: The challenge of creating high-quality and original digital products that stand out in a competitive market. The need for consistent marketing efforts to drive traffic and generate sales for your digital products. The potential for piracy or unauthorized distribution of your digital products, impacting your revenue and intellectual property rights. The responsibility of handling customer inquiries, refunds, and technical support related to your digital products. The possibility of facing fluctuating demand for specific digital products or niches.

Tips: Identify a niche or area of expertise that aligns with your skills and interests, making it easier to create valuable and authentic digital products. Conduct market research to understand customer needs and preferences, ensuring your products meet their requirements. Offer free samples or trials to attract potential customers and build trust in the quality of your digital products. Leverage social media and email marketing to promote your digital products and engage with your audience. Collaborate with influencers or other creators to expand your reach and tap into new customer bases.

Do's: Invest in professional design software or templates to create visually appealing digital products. Provide clear and informative product descriptions to communicate the value and benefits of your offerings. Offer customer support and assistance to address inquiries or technical issues promptly. Collaborate with other creators or brands to create bundle offers or cross-promotional opportunities. Regularly update and improve your digital products based on customer feedback and market trends.

Don'ts: Avoid using copyrighted material or infringing on intellectual property rights when creating digital products. Don't overprice your digital products, as competitive pricing can attract more customers and drive sales. Avoid neglecting marketing efforts; consistent promotion is essential for generating sales and increasing revenue. Don't compromise on the quality of your digital products to expedite the creation process. Avoid misleading marketing tactics or false advertising, as they can harm your reputation and customer trust.

In conclusion, starting a side hustle involving the creation and sale of digital products offers an exciting opportunity to showcase your creativity and expertise while generating passive income. By honing your content creation and design skills, understanding your target audience, and implementing effective marketing strategies, you can establish a successful venture in the digital product market. Embrace the challenges and remain open to learning and refining your digital product offerings to optimize your profit potential. With dedication, creativity, and customer-centric approach, your digital product side hustle can flourish, offering you the opportunity for financial success and a fulfilling entrepreneurial journey.

## 29. Selling second-hand books or vintage items online

Before diving into the world of selling second-hand books or vintage items online as a side hustle, it's crucial to equip yourself with the necessary knowledge, financial considerations, and an understanding of the profit potential in the online resale market. In this comprehensive guide, we will explore the expertise needed, financial aspects, profit potential, pros and cons, and essential tips, do's, and don'ts to help you establish a successful venture in selling second-hand books or vintage items online. Let's delve into the details!

Knowledge Needed: Familiarize yourself with the online resale market, identifying popular platforms and marketplaces for second-hand books and vintage items. Acquire knowledge of book or vintage item valuation, condition grading, and pricing to ensure fair and competitive selling. Understand copyright laws and intellectual property rights to avoid legal issues related to selling books or vintage items. Stay updated with trends, collectibles, and demand in the resale market to make informed purchasing decisions.

Money Needed: Starting an online resale side hustle can be relatively affordable, but some initial investment may be required. Budget for sourcing second-hand books or vintage items, shipping materials, and online platform fees. Allocate funds for marketing and promotion to attract potential buyers to your online store or listings. Consider investing in online courses or resources to enhance your knowledge of book or vintage item valuation and identification.

Profit Potential: The profit potential in selling second-hand books or vintage items online can be promising, provided you source valuable and sought-after items and effectively market your offerings. Earnings are based on the resale price minus the initial cost and associated fees. Profit potential can be maximized by sourcing unique or rare items, building a loyal customer base, and implementing effective pricing and marketing strategies.

Pros: The opportunity to turn a passion for books or vintage items into a profitable side hustle. The potential for passive income, as online listings can attract buyers even when you're not actively selling. The ability to reach a global audience through online platforms, expanding your customer base. The chance to explore various niche markets within the resale industry, catering to specific interests and demands. The satisfaction of preserving and appreciating vintage items while finding them new homes.

Cons: The challenge of sourcing high-quality and valuable second-hand books or vintage items at reasonable prices. The need for effective inventory management to keep track of available items and prevent overselling. The potential competition from other sellers, especially in popular or niche markets. The responsibility of packing and shipping items promptly and securely to maintain customer satisfaction. The possibility of facing fluctuations in demand or sales based on market trends and seasonality.

Tips: Specialize in a particular niche or category of second-hand books or vintage items to stand out in the market and attract a specific audience. Offer detailed and accurate item descriptions, including condition, history, and any unique features, to build trust with potential buyers. Provide high-quality photographs that showcase the items from different angles, enabling buyers to make informed decisions. Price your items competitively, considering factors such as rarity, condition, and market demand.

Do's: Regularly update your online store or listings with new and fresh inventory to keep customers engaged. Participate in online communities, forums, or social media groups related to book or vintage item collecting to connect with potential buyers. Offer excellent customer service, promptly responding to inquiries and addressing any issues that may arise. Package items securely to prevent damage during shipping and deliver them in a timely manner.

Don'ts: Avoid misrepresenting the condition or history of second-hand books or vintage items to maintain transparency and trust with buyers. Don't overprice items, as it may deter potential buyers and impact your reputation as a seller. Avoid neglecting customer feedback or reviews; learn from feedback to improve your services and offerings. Don't hoard inventory; keep your online store or listings updated with new items and remove sold items promptly.

In conclusion, starting a side hustle involving the sale of second-hand books or vintage items online offers an exciting opportunity to turn a passion for collecting into a profitable venture. By acquiring the necessary knowledge of the resale market, sourcing valuable items, and implementing effective marketing strategies, you can establish a successful online resale business. Embrace the challenges and remain open to learning and adapting your strategies to optimize your profit potential. With dedication, a keen eye for valuable items, and excellent customer service, your online resale side hustle can flourish, offering you the opportunity for financial success and a fulfilling journey in the world of vintage item selling.

## 30. Offering resume writing or career coaching services

Before delving into the world of offering resume writing or career coaching services as a side hustle, it's essential to equip yourself with the necessary knowledge, financial considerations, and an understanding of the profit potential in the career services market. In this comprehensive guide, we will explore the expertise needed, financial aspects, profit potential, pros and cons, and essential tips, do's, and don'ts to help you establish a successful venture in offering resume writing or career coaching services. Let's delve into the details!

Knowledge Needed: Familiarize yourself with the current job market trends, hiring practices, and industry-specific requirements to offer relevant and tailored career services. Acquire expertise in resume writing techniques, cover letter crafting, and interview coaching to assist clients effectively. Understand various career paths and industries to provide valuable career guidance and coaching. Stay updated with job search strategies, networking techniques, and digital platforms to assist clients in their career advancement.

Money Needed: Starting a career services side hustle may require minimal initial investment, but some costs should be considered. Budget for marketing expenses to promote your services and reach potential clients. Allocate funds for professional development, such as attending workshops or obtaining certifications to enhance your expertise. Consider investing in software or tools for resume writing and career coaching.

Profit Potential: The profit potential in offering resume writing or career coaching services can be promising, provided you offer high-quality and results-driven services. Earnings are typically based on the fees charged for resume writing, career coaching sessions, or packaged service offerings. Profit potential can be maximized by building a strong client base, gaining positive testimonials, and establishing a reputable brand in the career services industry.

Pros: The opportunity to make a meaningful impact on individuals' careers by helping them secure better job opportunities. The potential for recurring business, as clients may seek additional career services throughout their professional journey. The ability to work remotely and set your own schedule, offering flexibility and work-life balance. The satisfaction of witnessing clients succeed in their job search or career progression with your guidance. The chance to explore various niches within the career services market, such as resume writing for specific industries or executive coaching.

Cons: The challenge of differentiating yourself in a competitive market with numerous career coaches and resume writers. The need for ongoing marketing efforts to attract and retain clients in the competitive career services industry. The responsibility of managing client expectations and ensuring timely delivery of services. The potential for emotional involvement, as career coaching may require providing support during clients' job search or career transitions. The possibility of facing fluctuations in client demand based on job market conditions or economic trends.

Tips: Identify your unique selling points and areas of expertise to stand out in the career services market. Offer a variety of service packages to cater to different client needs and budgets. Develop a professional online presence, including a website and active social media profiles, to showcase your expertise and attract potential clients. Leverage networking opportunities to connect with potential clients and build professional relationships in your target industries.

Do's: Offer personalized and customized career advice and services to address each client's unique career goals and challenges. Stay up-to-date with industry trends, job search techniques, and resume best practices to offer relevant and effective guidance. Seek feedback from clients to continuously improve your services and meet their expectations. Set clear and realistic goals with clients and track their progress during career coaching sessions.

Cultivate a positive and supportive coaching approach to empower clients in their career journey.

Don'ts: Avoid making unrealistic promises or guarantees of job placements to maintain transparency and integrity in your services. Don't overlook the importance of confidentiality; ensure that client information and career discussions remain private and secure. Avoid overbooking your schedule to ensure that you can dedicate ample time and attention to each client. Don't rely solely on one marketing channel; diversify your marketing efforts to reach a broader audience.

In conclusion, starting a side hustle in offering resume writing or career coaching services provides a fulfilling opportunity to positively impact individuals' careers and help them achieve their professional goals. By acquiring the necessary knowledge in career services, staying updated with industry trends, and implementing effective marketing strategies, you can establish a successful venture in the career coaching industry. Embrace the challenges and remain committed to delivering exceptional services to clients. With dedication, empathy, and a client-centric approach, your career services side hustle can flourish, offering you the opportunity for financial success and a rewarding journey in assisting others in their career advancement.

## 31. Renting out camping spaces on your property

Before embarking on a side hustle of renting out camping spaces on your property, it is vital to equip yourself with the necessary knowledge, financial considerations, and an understanding of the profit potential in the camping rental market. In this comprehensive guide, we will explore the expertise needed, financial aspects, profit potential, pros and cons, and essential tips, do's, and don'ts to help you establish a successful venture in renting out camping spaces on your property. Let's delve into the details!

Knowledge Needed: Familiarize yourself with local zoning and land-use regulations to ensure you can legally offer camping spaces on your property. Understand safety and liability considerations, such as providing appropriate amenities and addressing potential hazards. Acquire knowledge of the camping market, including popular camping destinations, target demographics, and seasonal demand. Familiarize yourself with campground management, customer service, and reservation systems to create a positive camping experience for guests.

Money Needed: Starting a camping rental side hustle may require some initial investment to set up the camping spaces and necessary amenities. Budget for essential camping equipment such as tents, sleeping bags, and campfire supplies. Allocate funds for maintaining the camping area, providing restroom facilities, and ensuring a safe environment for guests. Consider investing in advertising and marketing to attract campers to your property.

Profit Potential: The profit potential in renting out camping spaces on your property can be promising, especially during peak camping seasons and in popular camping destinations. Earnings are typically based on the fees charged per camping space per night. Profit potential can be maximized by offering unique camping experiences, providing exceptional customer service, and effectively marketing your camping rental.

Pros: The opportunity to generate passive income by utilizing your property for camping rentals. The chance to connect with nature enthusiasts and travelers from diverse backgrounds. The potential to build a loyal customer base and receive positive reviews and referrals. The flexibility to set your own availability and adjust pricing based on demand. The satisfaction of providing a memorable camping experience for guests and fostering a sense of community.

Cons: The responsibility of managing bookings, guest inquiries, and campsite maintenance. The need to address potential safety and security concerns to ensure a positive camping experience. The possibility of dealing with difficult guests or complaints, requiring effective conflict resolution skills. The challenge of marketing your camping spaces to attract a steady stream of campers. The potential impact of weather conditions on camping availability and cancellations.

Tips: Create a camping area that caters to different types of campers, such as tent sites, RV hookups, or glamping options. Offer additional amenities, such as picnic areas, campfire pits, or recreational activities, to enhance the camping experience. Provide clear and detailed information on your website or listing regarding camping rules, check-in procedures, and available facilities. Consider partnering with local outdoor activity providers or offering guided tours to add value to the camping experience.

Do's: Ensure your camping spaces are clean, well-maintained, and equipped with necessary amenities. Respond promptly to camper inquiries and booking requests to provide excellent customer service. Promote sustainable camping practices and educate guests on Leave No Trace principles. Encourage guests to leave reviews and share their camping experiences on social media to attract more campers. Regularly inspect the camping area for potential safety hazards and address them promptly.

Don'ts: Avoid overbooking your camping spaces, ensuring you have sufficient availability for each reservation. Don't neglect camper feedback or complaints; use them as opportunities for improvement. Avoid hosting events or activities that may disturb other campers' experience without their consent. Don't neglect advertising and marketing efforts, as attracting new campers is crucial for sustained business growth. Avoid compromising safety or liability standards to cut costs.

In conclusion, starting a side hustle of renting out camping spaces on your property offers an exciting opportunity to earn passive income while sharing your love for the outdoors with travelers and nature enthusiasts. By acquiring the necessary knowledge in campground management, ensuring safety and liability compliance, and providing exceptional customer service, you can establish a successful venture in camping rentals. Embrace the challenges and remain committed to delivering a memorable and enjoyable camping experience for your guests. With dedication, attention to detail, and a passion for camping, your camping rental side hustle can thrive, offering you the opportunity for financial success and a rewarding journey in the world of outdoor hospitality.

## 32. Launching an online course or membership site

Before venturing into the side hustle of launching an online course or membership site, it is essential to equip yourself with the necessary knowledge, financial considerations, and an understanding of the profit potential in the online education market. In this comprehensive guide, we will explore the expertise needed, financial aspects, profit potential, pros and cons, and essential tips, do's, and don'ts to help you establish a successful venture in creating and selling online courses or membership sites. Let's delve into the details!

Knowledge Needed: Familiarize yourself with the subject matter or expertise you plan to teach in your online course or membership site. Acquire knowledge in instructional design and curriculum development to create engaging and effective educational content. Understand different e-learning platforms and technologies to choose the most suitable platform for hosting your online course or membership site. Familiarize yourself with online marketing and audience targeting strategies to attract potential learners to your educational offerings.

Money Needed: Starting an online course or membership site side hustle may require some initial investment, depending on the scale and complexity of your educational platform. Budget for video and audio recording equipment, course development software, and graphic design tools. Allocate funds for website hosting, domain registration, and e-learning platform fees. Consider investing in online advertising and promotions to reach a broader audience.

Profit Potential: The profit potential in launching an online course or membership site can be promising, especially if you offer valuable and sought-after educational content. Earnings are typically based on course enrollment fees or recurring membership subscriptions. Profit potential can be maximized by continuously updating and improving your educational content, growing your audience, and expanding your course offerings.

Pros: The opportunity to share your knowledge and expertise with a global audience, making a positive impact on learners' lives. The potential for passive income, as online courses and membership sites can generate revenue even when you're not actively teaching. The ability to scale your business by enrolling multiple learners in your courses or memberships simultaneously. The flexibility to set your own course schedule and update content based on learner feedback. The satisfaction of witnessing learners' growth and success through your educational offerings.

Cons: The challenge of creating high-quality and engaging educational content that meets learners' expectations. The need for ongoing marketing efforts to attract new learners and maintain member retention. The potential for competition in the online education market, requiring you to differentiate your courses from similar offerings. The responsibility of managing technical aspects of your e-learning platform and addressing any technical issues that may arise.

Tips: Choose a niche or subject matter that aligns with your expertise and passion, ensuring you can offer valuable and engaging content. Utilize multimedia elements, such as videos, quizzes, and interactive exercises, to enhance the learning experience. Offer free or discounted trial periods to attract new learners and allow them to sample your educational content. Implement a feedback system to gather learner insights and continuously improve your courses or membership offerings.

Do's: Promote your online courses or membership site through various channels, such as social media, email marketing, and partnerships. Engage with your learners regularly through discussion forums or live Q&A sessions to foster a sense of community. Provide exceptional customer support and address any learner inquiries or issues promptly. Keep your educational content up-to-date and relevant to reflect industry trends and advancements. Offer certificates or badges to learners upon course completion to boost learner motivation.

Don'ts: Avoid overpricing your online courses or membership subscriptions, as it may deter potential learners. Don't neglect marketing efforts or assume learners will find your courses on their own. Avoid sacrificing quality for quantity; focus on creating in-depth and comprehensive educational content. Don't promise unrealistic results to learners, but instead emphasize the knowledge and skills they will acquire.

In conclusion, launching an online course or membership site provides an exciting opportunity to share your expertise, generate passive income, and impact learners worldwide. By acquiring the necessary knowledge in instructional design, leveraging e-learning technologies, and implementing effective marketing strategies, you can establish a successful venture in online education. Embrace the challenges and remain committed to delivering high-quality educational content that meets learners' needs. With dedication, continuous improvement, and a passion for teaching, your online course or membership site side hustle can flourish, offering you the opportunity for financial success and a rewarding journey in the world of online education.

## 33. Creating and selling custom jewelry or accessories

Before delving into the side hustle of creating and selling custom jewelry or accessories, it's crucial to arm yourself with the necessary knowledge, financial considerations, and an understanding of the profit potential in the jewelry market. In this comprehensive guide, we will explore the expertise needed, financial aspects, profit potential, pros and cons, and essential tips, do's, and don'ts to help you establish a successful venture in custom jewelry or accessory design and sales. Let's explore the details!

Knowledge Needed: Familiarize yourself with different jewelry-making techniques, such as wire wrapping, beading, metalwork, or resin casting, depending on the style of custom jewelry you aim to create. Acquire knowledge of various jewelry materials and gemstones, their properties, and where to source high-quality supplies. Understand current jewelry trends and customer preferences to design pieces that appeal to your target audience. Familiarize yourself with online platforms and marketplaces for selling custom jewelry, as well as marketing and branding strategies to promote your products effectively.

Money Needed: Starting a custom jewelry or accessory side hustle may require an initial investment to purchase tools, materials, and supplies. Budget for jewelry-making tools, such as pliers, wire cutters, and a jewelry torch, if necessary. Allocate funds for purchasing gemstones, beads, metals, and findings to create your custom pieces. Consider investing in professional photography equipment to showcase your jewelry attractively. Factor in packaging materials and shipping costs if you plan to sell online.

Profit Potential: The profit potential in creating and selling custom jewelry or accessories can be rewarding, especially if you offer unique and high-quality pieces that resonate with customers. Earnings are typically based on the pricing of your custom jewelry, and profit potential can be maximized by building a strong brand identity, expanding your customer base, and offering personalized designs.

Pros: The opportunity to express your creativity and design unique pieces that reflect your artistic vision. The potential to build a loyal customer base who appreciate handmade and custom jewelry. The flexibility to work from home and set your own schedule, making it an ideal side hustle for those with other commitments. The satisfaction of seeing customers delighted with their personalized jewelry and accessories. The potential for growth and expansion, such as offering custom designs for special occasions or collaborating with other artisans.

Cons: The challenge of competing with mass-produced and lower-priced jewelry in the market. The time-consuming nature of handmade jewelry, especially for intricate designs. The responsibility of managing inventory, orders, and shipping, especially during busy periods. The need for ongoing marketing efforts to attract customers and stand out in a competitive market. The potential for fluctuations in demand, depending on seasonal trends and consumer preferences.

Tips: Find your unique niche or style that sets your custom jewelry apart from others in the market. Offer personalized jewelry options, such as initial necklaces, birthstone rings, or custom engravings, to cater to individual preferences. Utilize social media platforms and create a visually appealing website or online store to showcase your jewelry designs effectively. Collaborate with influencers or jewelry enthusiasts to reach a broader audience and gain exposure for your brand. Attend local craft fairs or jewelry exhibitions to connect with potential customers and gain valuable feedback.

Do's: Invest in high-quality materials and craftsmanship to create durable and attractive custom jewelry. Offer excellent customer service, responding promptly to inquiries and fulfilling orders in a timely manner. Use high-resolution images and accurate product descriptions to represent your jewelry accurately online. Create a cohesive brand identity, including a logo and packaging, to build a professional image for your jewelry business. Continuously update your jewelry collection to reflect current trends and customer preferences.

Don'ts: Avoid compromising on the quality of your custom jewelry to cut costs, as this can tarnish your brand reputation. Don't overprice your jewelry; research the market and competitor pricing to set fair and competitive prices. Avoid relying solely on one sales channel; explore multiple platforms and avenues to diversify your sales. Don't neglect marketing efforts; consistent promotion is essential to attract new customers and retain existing ones. Avoid copying or imitating other designers' work; focus on developing your unique style and artistic vision.

In conclusion, creating and selling custom jewelry or accessories offers an exciting opportunity to express your creativity, connect with customers, and generate income through your artistic talent. By acquiring the necessary knowledge in jewelry-making techniques, sourcing quality materials, and adopting effective marketing strategies, you can establish a successful venture in custom jewelry design and sales. Embrace the challenges and remain committed to delivering high-quality and personalized pieces that resonate with your customers. With dedication, passion, and a strong focus on customer satisfaction, your custom jewelry side hustle can thrive, offering you the opportunity for financial success and a rewarding journey in the world of artisanal craftsmanship.

## 34. Offering mobile phone repair services

Before embarking on the side hustle of offering mobile phone repair services, it is vital to understand the knowledge required, financial considerations, and profit potential in the mobile phone repair industry. In this comprehensive guide, we will explore the expertise needed, financial aspects, profit potential, pros and cons, and essential tips, do's, and don'ts to help you establish a successful venture in mobile phone repair services. Let's delve into the details!

Knowledge Needed: Acquire technical knowledge and skills in mobile phone repair, including diagnosing common issues, replacing damaged components, and conducting software troubleshooting. Familiarize yourself with different smartphone models and their specifications to cater to a broad range of customers. Stay updated on the latest mobile phone technologies and trends, as the industry evolves rapidly. Understanding the use of specialized tools and equipment is essential for efficient and accurate repairs.

Additionally, knowledge of safety protocols and handling hazardous materials during repairs is crucial.

Money Needed: Starting a mobile phone repair side hustle may require an initial investment in acquiring repair tools, spare parts, and equipment. Budget for essential repair tools like screwdrivers, tweezers, and spudgers. Allocate funds for purchasing high-quality replacement parts from reputable suppliers. Consider investing in diagnostic software and device-specific testing equipment to enhance your repair capabilities. Factor in costs for marketing and advertising to reach potential customers effectively.

Profit Potential: The profit potential in offering mobile phone repair services can be significant, given the ubiquitous nature of smartphones and their frequent need for repairs. Earnings are typically based on the fees charged for each repair, and profit potential can be maximized by providing timely and reliable services, fostering customer loyalty, and exploring additional revenue streams, such as selling accessories or offering device trade-in services.

Pros: The opportunity to capitalize on the growing demand for mobile phone repairs due to increased smartphone usage. The ability to offer a valuable service that helps customers extend the lifespan of their devices. The potential for repeat business and word-of-mouth referrals when providing excellent customer service. The flexibility to set your own working hours and operate as a mobile repair service, allowing you to reach customers at their convenience. The satisfaction of solving technical challenges and helping customers regain functionality in their devices.

Cons: The need to stay up-to-date with rapidly evolving mobile phone technologies and repair methods. The risk of accidentally causing further damage to a customer's device during repairs, leading to potential liability issues. The challenge of competing with larger repair franchises and online repair services. The potential for slower business during periods of economic downturn or reduced consumer spending. The responsibility of handling sensitive customer data and ensuring privacy and security during repairs.

Tips: Offer a diverse range of repair services to cater to different phone models and issues, increasing your customer base. Provide transparent pricing and cost estimates upfront to build trust with customers. Offer warranty options on repairs to assure customers of the quality and reliability of your services. Focus on exceptional customer service, responding promptly to inquiries and addressing any post-repair issues promptly. Build a strong online presence through a professional website and active social media channels to reach a broader audience.

Do's: Invest in high-quality replacement parts from reputable suppliers to ensure the durability of repairs. Keep accurate records of repairs, customer interactions, and warranty information for efficient business management. Offer value-added services, such as screen protectors or phone accessories, to increase revenue and enhance the customer experience. Emphasize honesty and transparency when advising customers on whether repairs are cost-effective or if a device should be replaced. Regularly update your knowledge and skills through workshops, online courses, and industry certifications.

Don'ts: Don't compromise on the quality of repair work to cut costs, as it can lead to dissatisfied customers and negative reviews. Avoid rushing repairs; take the time needed to ensure accurate and thorough diagnoses and repairs. Don't overcharge customers for simple repairs; maintain fair and competitive pricing to build customer loyalty. Avoid neglecting customer feedback and online reviews; use them to improve your services and address any concerns promptly. Don't attempt complex repairs without proper training or expertise; refer customers to specialists or authorized repair centers when necessary.

In conclusion, offering mobile phone repair services can be a lucrative and rewarding side hustle, provided you possess the technical knowledge, financial resources, and commitment to customer satisfaction. By continually updating your repair skills, investing in quality tools and parts, and providing excellent customer service, you can build a successful venture in the mobile phone repair industry. Embrace the challenges and maintain a strong focus on delivering reliable and efficient repairs to build a loyal customer base. With dedication, professionalism, and a passion for helping customers, your mobile phone repair side hustle can thrive, offering you the potential for financial success and a fulfilling journey in the world of mobile technology services.

## 35. Providing transcription services

Before embarking on the side hustle of providing transcription services, it is essential to understand the knowledge required, financial considerations, and profit potential in the transcription industry. In this comprehensive guide, we will explore the expertise needed, financial aspects, profit potential, pros and cons, and essential tips, do's, and don'ts to help you establish a successful venture in transcription services. Let's delve into the details!

Knowledge Needed: To excel in providing transcription services, you must have excellent language skills, including grammar, punctuation, and spelling. Proficiency in the language you are transcribing (e.g., English) is crucial to ensure accuracy and clarity in the final transcript. Familiarity with specialized terminologies, depending on the field you'll be transcribing for, such as medical, legal, or technical jargon, may be necessary. An understanding of audio editing software and transcription tools can streamline the process and improve efficiency. Strong attention to detail and the ability to work efficiently under tight deadlines are essential attributes for a successful transcriptionist.

Money Needed: Starting a transcription service side hustle may require minimal initial investment. Basic transcription software and tools are often available for free or at affordable prices. However, if you plan to transcribe audio files professionally, investing in quality transcription software can enhance productivity. Additionally, consider budgeting for ongoing professional development courses to further improve your transcription skills.

Profit Potential: The profit potential in offering transcription services can be substantial, depending on the volume of work you undertake and the rates you charge. Transcription fees are typically based on factors such as the length of the audio/video file, the difficulty of the content, and turnaround time. The ability to transcribe efficiently and accurately can lead to higher earnings as you take on more projects and build a strong client base. Specializing in niche fields with high demand, such as medical or legal transcription, can also command premium rates.

Pros: Flexible working hours, allowing you to schedule transcription tasks around your existing commitments. The opportunity to work from home or any location with an internet connection, offering convenience and reduced commuting expenses. The potential for a diverse range of clients and projects, ranging from academic research to business meetings. The satisfaction of contributing to various industries by providing accurate and accessible transcripts. The possibility of scaling your transcription business by hiring subcontractors or building a team.

Cons: The need to stay focused and maintain productivity, as transcription can be time-consuming, especially for lengthy audio files. The risk of encountering poor audio quality or challenging accents, which may impact the accuracy of the transcription. The potential for repetitive strain injuries or eye strain due to prolonged computer use during transcription. The challenge of building a steady client base initially, which may require networking and marketing efforts. The responsibility of handling confidential information in certain transcription projects, necessitating strict data security measures.

Tips: Start with transcription projects in areas where you have expertise or familiarity to build confidence and accuracy. Practice regularly to improve typing speed and accuracy, enabling you to handle more projects efficiently. Use good quality headphones to improve audio clarity and reduce errors caused by background noise. Invest in transcription software that offers playback controls and keyboard shortcuts for enhanced productivity. Develop a professional website or online portfolio to showcase your transcription services and attract potential clients.

Do's: Maintain open communication with clients, seeking clarifications when necessary to ensure accurate transcriptions. Deliver transcriptions within agreed-upon deadlines to build a reputation for reliability. Proofread your transcriptions thoroughly to eliminate errors and deliver high-quality work. Offer competitive and fair pricing based on the complexity of the transcription task and your expertise. Continuously update your transcription skills and knowledge to stay competitive in the industry.

Don'ts: Don't accept transcription projects with tight deadlines if you are unsure of delivering quality work within the given time frame. Avoid taking on projects with subject matter or specialized terminologies you are not familiar with, as it may compromise accuracy. Don't rely solely on automated transcription software, as human intervention is essential for context and accuracy. Avoid transcribing in distracting environments to maintain focus and deliver error-free transcriptions. Don't ignore client feedback; use it to improve your services and build lasting relationships.

In conclusion, providing transcription services as a side hustle offers a flexible and potentially lucrative opportunity for individuals with strong language skills and attention to detail. By investing in the right tools, continuously improving your transcription skills, and delivering reliable and accurate transcriptions, you can build a successful transcription business. Offering specialized transcription services in high-demand fields can open doors to premium rates and a steady stream of projects. Embrace the challenges, remain committed to delivering top-notch services, and leverage technology to streamline your transcription process. With dedication and professionalism, your transcription side hustle can flourish, providing both financial rewards and a fulfilling career in the transcription industry.

## 36. Offering online language tutoring

Before delving into the side hustle of offering online language tutoring, it's essential to understand the necessary knowledge, financial considerations, and profit potential in this field. In this comprehensive guide, we will explore the expertise required, financial aspects, profit potential, pros and cons, and essential tips, do's, and don'ts to help you establish a successful online language tutoring venture. Let's dive into the details!

Knowledge Needed: To excel in online language tutoring, you must possess strong language proficiency in the language you plan to teach. Native or near-native fluency is often preferred to provide authentic language instruction. Additionally, you should have a solid understanding of grammar, vocabulary, pronunciation, and cultural nuances. Knowledge of effective teaching methodologies and language learning strategies is crucial to design engaging and impactful lessons. Familiarity with online teaching platforms and tools, such as video conferencing software and interactive whiteboards, is essential for delivering seamless virtual tutoring sessions. Being patient, empathetic, and adaptable will contribute to a positive learning experience for your students.

Money Needed: Starting an online language tutoring side hustle may require minimal initial investment. You will need a reliable computer, a stable internet connection, and a good quality headset with a microphone for clear communication. Some online teaching platforms may have associated fees for membership or usage, so consider these costs while planning your budget. You may also choose to invest in supplementary teaching materials, language textbooks, or language learning software to enhance the learning experience for your students.

Profit Potential: The profit potential in offering online language tutoring can be substantial, depending on factors such as your expertise, the language's demand, and the rates you charge. As you build a strong reputation and gain positive reviews from satisfied students, you can increase your hourly rates. Specializing in niche languages or catering to specific language learning needs, such as business language or exam preparation, can command premium rates. Additionally, offering group lessons or package deals may increase your earnings and attract more students.

Pros: Flexible working hours, allowing you to schedule tutoring sessions around your existing commitments. The opportunity to reach a global audience of language learners, transcending geographical boundaries. The ability to tailor lessons to meet individual student needs, providing personalized learning experiences. The satisfaction of helping students achieve their language learning goals and witnessing their progress. The potential for repeat business and referrals as satisfied students recommend your tutoring services to others.

Cons: The challenge of managing time zones and accommodating students from different parts of the world. The potential for technical issues or internet connectivity problems during virtual tutoring sessions. Competition from other online language tutors, requiring you to stand out by offering unique teaching approaches or specialized language courses. The need to continuously update your teaching methods and stay informed about language learning trends and resources. The possibility of encountering unmotivated or disengaged students, necessitating creative approaches to keep them engaged.

Tips: Identify your target audience and tailor your language tutoring services to meet their specific needs and goals.

Develop a well-structured curriculum with clear learning objectives for each lesson or course. Incorporate interactive and engaging activities to maintain student interest and facilitate active language practice. Utilize multimedia resources, such as videos, podcasts, and online language games, to make learning enjoyable and diverse. Encourage regular practice outside of tutoring sessions and provide constructive feedback to help students improve.

Do's: Establish a professional online presence through a website or social media platforms to showcase your language tutoring services. Offer a free trial lesson or introductory session to attract potential students and demonstrate your teaching approach. Maintain open communication with your students, addressing their questions and concerns promptly. Encourage a positive and inclusive learning environment, promoting cultural understanding and respect. Continuously seek feedback from students to improve your teaching methods and adapt to their needs.

Don'ts: Don't overcommit to too many students or tutoring hours, as it may lead to burnout and compromise the quality of your teaching. Avoid using a one-size-fits-all approach; instead, tailor your lessons to accommodate the unique learning styles of your students. Don't promise unrealistic language learning outcomes or guaranteed fluency within a short period. Avoid being inflexible with your teaching methods; be open to trying new approaches based on student feedback and learning outcomes. Don't neglect marketing efforts; actively promote your language tutoring services to attract new students.

In conclusion, offering online language tutoring can be a rewarding and profitable side hustle for individuals with strong language skills and a passion for teaching. By investing in the right tools, continuously improving your teaching methods, and providing personalized learning experiences, you can build a successful online tutoring business. Specializing in niche languages or catering to specific language learning needs can set you apart from competitors and attract a dedicated student base. Embrace the challenges and opportunities of online language tutoring, and foster a positive learning environment to help your students achieve their language learning goals. With dedication and commitment to delivering high-quality instruction, your online language tutoring side hustle can thrive and contribute to the language learning journey of students worldwide.

## 37. Creating and selling personalized gifts

Before embarking on the side hustle of creating and selling personalized gifts, it's essential to understand the required knowledge, financial considerations, and profit potential in this field. In this comprehensive guide, we will explore the expertise needed, financial aspects, profit potential, pros and cons, and essential tips, do's, and don'ts to help you establish a successful personalized gifts business. Let's delve into the details!

Knowledge Needed: To excel in creating and selling personalized gifts, you should have a good understanding of various crafting techniques and materials. Knowledge of design principles and aesthetics will help you create visually appealing and unique gift items. Familiarity with digital design software and printing methods is crucial for customizing gifts. Additionally, market research will be beneficial to identify popular trends and customer preferences. Having good communication skills is essential for understanding your customers' requirements and providing personalized solutions. Furthermore, knowledge of packaging and shipping methods will ensure safe delivery of your products to customers.

Money Needed: Starting a personalized gifts side hustle may require a moderate initial investment, depending on the scale of your business and the materials you use. You'll need to purchase crafting supplies, printing equipment (if applicable), packaging materials, and perhaps invest in a website or online store to showcase your products. Marketing expenses, such as promotional materials or social media advertising, may also be considered. As your business grows, you can reinvest profits to expand your product range and enhance your offerings.

Profit Potential: The profit potential in creating and selling personalized gifts can be significant, especially if you cater to niche markets or offer unique, high-quality products. Customized gifts often command higher prices than mass-produced items, allowing you to achieve higher profit margins. Building a loyal customer base through exceptional customer service and personalized offerings can lead to repeat business and referrals. Participating in seasonal markets, events, and online platforms can further boost sales and profitability.

Pros: The joy of turning your creative passion into a profitable venture and making meaningful connections with customers through personalized gifts. Flexibility in designing and producing a wide range of gift items, from custom mugs and apparel to engraved jewelry and home decor. The potential to offer personalized gifts for various occasions, such as weddings, birthdays, anniversaries, and holidays. The ability to stand out in a competitive market by offering one-of-a-kind products that hold sentimental value for recipients. The opportunity to collaborate with customers to create truly special and unique gift items.

Cons: The time-consuming nature of creating personalized gifts, especially for large orders or intricate designs. The challenge of managing inventory and ensuring timely delivery of customized items, especially during peak seasons. The need to stay updated with market trends and customer preferences to remain relevant and appealing to potential buyers. The risk of facing competition from other personalized gift sellers, requiring you to continuously innovate and differentiate your products. The potential for occasional design revisions or unsatisfied customers, necessitating effective communication and problem-solving skills.

Tips: Identify your target audience and tailor your personalized gift offerings to their preferences and interests.

Offer a variety of customization options, such as font styles, color choices, and personalization messages, to cater to diverse customer needs. Showcase your product quality through high-resolution images and detailed product descriptions on your website or online store. Provide exceptional customer service by responding to inquiries promptly and addressing customer concerns professionally. Offer packaging options that reflect the sentimentality of personalized gifts, such as gift wrapping and custom messages.

Do's: Maintain a portfolio or product gallery on your website or social media platforms to showcase your previous works and attract potential customers. Keep track of popular occasions and events to create timely and relevant promotions for your personalized gift items. Collaborate with local businesses or event planners to expand your customer reach and offer corporate gifting services. Encourage customer reviews and testimonials to build trust and credibility with potential buyers. Stay open to feedback and customer suggestions to improve your products and customer experience continually.

Don'ts: Avoid overpricing your personalized gift items, as excessively high prices may deter potential customers. Don't compromise on the quality of materials and craftsmanship, as this directly impacts customer satisfaction. Avoid overcommitting to large orders without assessing your production capabilities and delivery timelines. Don't infringe on copyright or intellectual property rights when creating designs for personalized gifts. Avoid using poor-quality packaging or shipping methods that may lead to damaged products during transit.

In conclusion, starting a side hustle of creating and selling personalized gifts can be a fulfilling and financially rewarding venture. By harnessing your creativity and craftsmanship, you can offer unique and sentimental gift items that resonate with customers. Personalized gifts hold immense emotional value, making them sought-after commodities for various occasions. Through effective marketing, exceptional customer service, and continuous innovation, your personalized gifts business can flourish and bring joy to both you and your customers. Embrace the challenges and opportunities of this side hustle, and strive to make a meaningful impact in the lives of those who receive your heartfelt creations.

## 38. Running a local food delivery service

Before delving into the side hustle of running a local food delivery service, it's crucial to understand the necessary knowledge, financial considerations, and profit potential in this venture. In this comprehensive guide, we will explore the expertise needed, financial aspects, profit potential, pros and cons, and essential tips, do's, and don'ts to help you establish a successful local food delivery business. Let's get started!

Knowledge Needed: To excel in running a local food delivery service, you need a good understanding of the local food industry and consumer preferences. Knowledge of food safety regulations and proper handling practices is essential to ensure the safe delivery of meals. Familiarity with different cuisines and dietary preferences will help you cater to a diverse customer base. Understanding your target audience and identifying potential partners, such as restaurants and food vendors, is crucial for building strong business relationships. Additionally, knowledge of delivery logistics and efficient route planning will optimize your delivery operations.

Money Needed: Starting a local food delivery service requires moderate initial investment. You will need funds to establish your delivery infrastructure, such as purchasing delivery vehicles or partnering with third-party delivery services. Creating a user-friendly website or mobile app for order placement and payment processing may also incur development costs. Marketing expenses, such as online advertisements and promotional materials, are essential to attract customers. As your business grows, you can allocate funds to expand your delivery fleet and enhance your online presence.

Profit Potential: The profit potential in running a local food delivery service can be significant, especially in densely populated areas with high demand for convenient meal deliveries. By charging delivery fees or commission from partnering restaurants, you can generate revenue for each order fulfilled. Establishing partnerships with multiple restaurants and food vendors can increase your customer base and order volume, further boosting profitability. Offering timely and reliable delivery services, along with excellent customer service, will foster customer loyalty and encourage repeat business.

Pros: The opportunity to connect local restaurants and food vendors with a broader customer base, promoting local businesses. The potential for repeat business from satisfied customers, leading to steady revenue streams. Flexibility in operating hours, allowing you to cater to different mealtime demands, such as lunch and dinner. The ability to customize delivery services, including contactless delivery options and real-time order tracking. The potential to expand your delivery service to include groceries, catering, or specialty items, enhancing your service offerings.

Cons: The challenge of managing delivery logistics and ensuring on-time deliveries, especially during peak hours. The risk of facing stiff competition from established food delivery platforms, requiring you to offer unique value propositions. The need to address customer complaints or issues promptly to maintain a positive reputation. The potential for increased expenses during adverse weather conditions or unforeseen events that may disrupt delivery operations. The responsibility of ensuring food safety and quality during transportation, with possible liability in case of mishandling.

Tips: Focus on providing excellent customer service and quick response times to build trust and loyalty with customers. Collaborate with local restaurants and food vendors to offer exclusive deals and discounts, promoting mutual growth. Invest in efficient delivery tracking systems to keep customers informed about the status of their orders.

Offer a user-friendly online platform for seamless order placement and payment processing. Emphasize the importance of food safety and proper handling to all employees involved in the delivery process.

Do's: Regularly update your menu and offerings to cater to changing customer preferences and seasonal demands. Advertise your local food delivery service through social media, local publications, and partnerships with community organizations. Monitor customer feedback and reviews to identify areas for improvement and enhance your service quality. Implement a loyalty program or referral system to reward repeat customers and encourage word-of-mouth marketing. Comply with all food safety regulations and maintain hygiene standards during food handling and delivery.

Don'ts: Don't compromise on the quality of delivery service, as this directly impacts customer satisfaction and loyalty. Avoid overextending your delivery radius to ensure timely and reliable deliveries. Don't neglect marketing efforts, as raising awareness about your local food delivery service is essential for attracting customers. Avoid partnering with restaurants or food vendors with a history of poor customer reviews or quality issues. Don't overlook the importance of employee training in food handling and delivery protocols to maintain consistent service quality.

In conclusion, starting a local food delivery service offers a promising opportunity to connect local restaurants and food vendors with hungry customers seeking convenient meal options. By leveraging your knowledge of the local food industry and maintaining high-quality delivery services, you can establish a profitable and reputable business. Embrace the challenges and opportunities that come with this side hustle, and with dedication, innovation, and exceptional customer service, you can create a successful local food delivery service that satisfies appetites and builds strong community connections.

## 39. Providing IT support or computer repair services

Before embarking on a side hustle providing IT support or computer repair services, it's essential to understand the necessary knowledge, financial considerations, and profit potential in this field. In this comprehensive guide, we will explore the expertise required, financial aspects, profit potential, pros and cons, and essential tips, do's, and don'ts to help you establish a successful IT support and computer repair business. Let's delve into the details!

Knowledge Needed: To excel in providing IT support and computer repair services, you need a strong foundation in computer hardware and software. Understanding various operating systems, including Windows, macOS, and Linux, is crucial. Proficiency in diagnosing and troubleshooting hardware and software issues is essential to address customer problems effectively. Knowledge of networking principles and configurations will enable you to resolve connectivity and internet-related problems. Familiarity with cybersecurity practices will help protect clients' data and systems. Additionally, staying updated with the latest technological advancements in the IT industry is essential to offer cutting-edge solutions.

Money Needed: Starting an IT support and computer repair side hustle requires moderate initial investment. You'll need funds to acquire essential tools and diagnostic equipment for computer repair. Setting up a basic workstation and investing in licensed software for diagnostics and repair may also incur costs. Creating a professional website or online presence to attract customers may involve domain registration and hosting expenses. As your business grows, you can allocate funds to expand your service offerings and invest in advanced repair tools.

Profit Potential: The profit potential in providing IT support and computer repair services can be substantial, especially in areas with high demand for technical assistance. You can charge customers based on hourly rates for IT support or set fixed prices for specific repair services. Offering on-site repairs or remote support can increase customer convenience and satisfaction, leading to repeat business and positive word-of-mouth referrals. As businesses and individuals rely heavily on technology, a reputable IT support and computer repair service can lead to a steady flow of customers and profitable growth.

Pros: The opportunity to solve challenging technical problems and help customers overcome IT-related issues. The potential for repeat business and long-term client relationships, leading to a steady income stream. Flexibility in offering on-site or remote support, catering to diverse customer preferences. The ability to specialize in specific areas, such as data recovery, virus removal, or network setup, and become an expert in those domains. The option to expand your services to include small businesses, schools, or local organizations, broadening your customer base.

Cons: The challenge of keeping up with rapidly evolving technology and continuous learning to remain relevant in the IT industry. The potential for dealing with frustrated or impatient customers during high-stress technical emergencies. The risk of handling sensitive data during repairs, requiring strict confidentiality and data security measures. The responsibility of providing accurate diagnostics and repairs to avoid aggravating customers' computer issues. The potential for physical strain and long hours while conducting on-site repairs or handling multiple remote support sessions.

Tips: Provide excellent customer service by actively listening to customers' concerns and offering prompt and courteous assistance. Create a professional website or social media presence to showcase your expertise and attract potential clients. Offer competitive pricing and transparent billing practices to build trust with customers. Invest in high-quality diagnostic tools and software to deliver accurate and efficient repairs. Stay updated with the latest industry trends and certifications to enhance your credibility and skillset.

Do's: Advertise your IT support and computer repair services through local business directories, community forums, and social media platforms. Offer personalized solutions and recommendations based on customers' specific needs and budget constraints. Maintain detailed records of repairs, customer interactions, and feedback to improve your services continually. Collaborate with local businesses or educational institutions to establish mutually beneficial partnerships. Provide after-service support and follow-up to ensure customer satisfaction and address any post-repair issues promptly.

Don'ts: Don't compromise on the quality of repairs or IT support, as this can negatively impact your reputation and customer loyalty. Avoid overpromising on repair outcomes or turnaround times to manage customer expectations realistically. Don't overlook data protection and security measures during repairs, ensuring customer data remains confidential. Avoid engaging in unethical practices or recommending unnecessary upgrades or services to customers. Don't dismiss the importance of continuous learning and professional development to stay competitive in the IT industry.

In conclusion, starting a side hustle providing IT support and computer repair services offers a rewarding opportunity to assist individuals and businesses with their technical needs. By leveraging your knowledge and expertise in computer hardware, software, and networking, you can establish a reputable and profitable business. Embrace the challenges and opportunities that come with this venture, and with dedication, exceptional customer service, and continuous learning, you can build a successful IT support and computer repair service that meets the technological demands of today's world.

## 40. Providing marketing or SEO services

Before venturing into a side hustle providing marketing or SEO services, it's crucial to understand the necessary knowledge, financial aspects, and profit potential in this field. This comprehensive guide will explore the expertise required, financial considerations, profit potential, pros and cons, and essential tips, do's, and don'ts to help you establish a successful marketing and SEO service. Let's dive into the details!

Knowledge Needed: To excel in providing marketing or SEO services, you need a solid foundation in digital marketing concepts and strategies. Understanding search engine optimization (SEO) techniques, keyword research, and content optimization is essential to help clients improve their online visibility. Familiarity with social media marketing, email marketing, and online advertising will enable you to develop comprehensive marketing campaigns for businesses. Analytical skills to track and measure campaign performance are vital to provide data-driven recommendations. Staying up-to-date with industry trends and algorithm changes is crucial to offer effective and relevant marketing solutions.

Money Needed: Starting a marketing or SEO service as a side hustle requires moderate to significant initial investment. You'll need funds to set up a professional website, including domain registration and hosting costs. Investing in SEO tools, keyword research software, and analytics platforms may also incur expenses. Marketing campaigns may involve advertising costs, content creation, and graphic design fees. As your business grows, you may allocate funds for marketing initiatives to attract clients and expand your service offerings.

Profit Potential: The profit potential in providing marketing or SEO services can be substantial, as businesses increasingly rely on digital marketing for growth. You can charge clients based on hourly rates for consulting or offer package pricing for specific marketing services. Delivering measurable results and achieving tangible improvements in clients' online presence can lead to recurring business and referrals. As your reputation grows, you may attract larger clients and more significant projects, leading to increased profitability.

Pros: The opportunity to work with a diverse range of clients across various industries and niches. Flexibility in offering remote services, allowing you to cater to clients globally. The potential for recurring income through long-term marketing campaigns and ongoing SEO services. The ability to continuously learn and implement new marketing strategies and tactics. The satisfaction of seeing your efforts contribute to your clients' business success.

Cons: The competitive nature of the marketing and SEO industry, requiring you to distinguish yourself from other service providers. The challenge of managing multiple client projects simultaneously and meeting deadlines effectively.

140

The responsibility of delivering tangible results and meeting clients' expectations. The need to adapt to constantly evolving search engine algorithms and digital marketing trends. The potential for clients to have unrealistic expectations regarding immediate results.

Tips: Build a strong online presence and showcase your expertise through a professional website and portfolio. Stay informed about the latest marketing and SEO trends by reading industry blogs and attending webinars and conferences. Offer a comprehensive initial consultation to understand clients' goals and tailor your services accordingly. Provide regular performance reports to clients to demonstrate the effectiveness of your marketing efforts. Network with other marketing professionals and potential clients through social media and professional platforms.

Do's: Do conduct thorough keyword research and competitor analysis to develop effective SEO strategies. Do implement ethical SEO practices and avoid black-hat techniques that may lead to penalties. Do establish clear communication channels with clients and be responsive to their inquiries. Do set realistic expectations with clients regarding the timeline and outcomes of marketing campaigns. Do invest in continuous learning and certifications to enhance your marketing skills.

Don'ts: Don't make promises of guaranteed rankings or immediate success, as SEO results require time and effort. Don't engage in spammy or unethical marketing practices that could harm your clients' reputations. Don't neglect to track and measure the performance of marketing campaigns to assess their effectiveness. Don't overextend yourself by taking on more clients than you can handle effectively. Don't shy away from seeking feedback from clients to improve your services continuously.

In conclusion, launching a side hustle providing marketing or SEO services offers an exciting opportunity to assist businesses in improving their online presence and achieving their marketing goals. By leveraging your knowledge and expertise in digital marketing and SEO, you can establish a reputable and profitable service. Embrace the challenges and opportunities in this dynamic industry, and with dedication, exceptional service, and continuous learning, you can build a successful marketing and SEO business that drives tangible results for your clients.

## 41. Providing drone photography and videography services

Before delving into a side hustle providing drone photography and videography services, it's essential to understand the required knowledge, financial considerations, profit potential, and various aspects of this venture. This comprehensive guide will explore the expertise needed, financial investment, profit potential, pros and cons, as well as valuable tips and do's and don'ts to help you establish a successful drone photography and videography business. Let's dive into the details!

Knowledge Needed: To excel in providing drone photography and videography services, you need a solid understanding of drone technology, including drone models and specifications suitable for photography and videography. Familiarity with drone laws and regulations in your country or region is vital to ensure compliance and safety during aerial operations. Learning how to operate a drone skillfully and capturing stunning aerial shots requires practice and experience. Acquiring knowledge in post-processing techniques for editing photos and videos will enhance the quality of your deliverables. Understanding composition and storytelling in photography and videography is crucial to create captivating and visually appealing content for clients.

Money Needed: Starting a drone photography and videography side hustle requires a significant initial investment in purchasing a high-quality drone suitable for professional photography and videography. Depending on your budget and specific requirements, the cost of a professional-grade drone can range from hundreds to thousands of dollars. Additionally, you may need to invest in extra batteries, memory cards, and protective equipment for your drone. Acquiring advanced editing software and a powerful computer for post-processing may also incur additional expenses. As your business grows, you might consider investing in marketing and advertising to expand your client base.

Profit Potential: The profit potential in providing drone photography and videography services can be substantial, as the demand for aerial content continues to rise in various industries. You can charge clients based on the complexity of the project, the number of deliverables, and the usage rights. Serving a diverse clientele, including real estate agents, event organizers, and businesses, can lead to a steady stream of income. As your reputation grows, you may attract larger projects and establish long-term partnerships, enhancing your profit potential significantly.

Pros: The opportunity to explore your creativity and capture unique and breathtaking aerial visuals. Flexibility in providing services for various industries, such as real estate, tourism, and advertising. The potential for recurring business through repeat clients and referrals. The ability to showcase your portfolio online and attract potential clients from different regions. The satisfaction of providing clients with stunning aerial imagery and adding value to their projects.

Cons: The significant initial investment in purchasing a high-quality drone and related equipment. The need to comply with drone regulations and restrictions, which may vary depending on location. The potential risk of accidents or damage to the drone during aerial operations. The challenge of differentiating your services in a competitive market and building a client base from scratch. The responsibility of ensuring data security and privacy when capturing and storing aerial content.

Tips: Invest in a reputable and reliable drone model with features suitable for professional photography and videography. Obtain the necessary licenses and permits required to operate a drone commercially in your area. Practice flying your drone in open spaces to improve your piloting skills and minimize accidents. Develop a strong portfolio showcasing various types of aerial shots to demonstrate your capabilities to potential clients. Network with professionals in related industries and attend local events to promote your services.

Do's: Do stay updated with the latest drone technology and regulations to ensure safe and compliant operations. Do collaborate with local businesses and photographers to expand your network and potential client base. Do offer customized packages and pricing options to cater to different client needs. Do communicate effectively with clients to understand their requirements and deliver content that meets their expectations. Do invest time in post-processing to enhance the quality and appeal of your aerial visuals.

Don'ts: Don't fly your drone in restricted or prohibited areas to avoid legal issues and penalties. Don't overlook the importance of obtaining liability insurance to protect yourself and your business from potential liabilities. Don't overcommit yourself by taking on more projects than you can handle, compromising the quality of your work. Don't neglect regular maintenance of your drone to ensure its optimal performance and longevity. Don't underestimate the power of marketing and branding to establish your drone photography and videography service in the market.

In conclusion, launching a side hustle providing drone photography and videography services offers an exciting opportunity to combine creativity and technology while serving diverse clients and industries. By acquiring the necessary knowledge, investing in quality equipment, and delivering exceptional aerial content, you can build a reputable and profitable business in the fast-growing field of drone photography and videography. Embrace the challenges and rewards of this venture, and with dedication and passion, you can soar high and create stunning visuals that leave a lasting impression on your clients.

## 42. Starting a specialty catering business (e.g., vegan, gluten-free)

Before embarking on a side hustle like starting a specialty catering business, focusing on a niche such as vegan or gluten-free catering, it's crucial to understand the necessary knowledge, financial requirements, profit potential, and various aspects of this venture. This comprehensive guide will explore the expertise needed, financial investment, profit potential, pros and cons, as well as valuable tips, do's, and don'ts to help you establish a successful specialty catering business. Let's dive into the details!

Knowledge Needed: Launching a specialty catering business demands in-depth knowledge of the specific niche you choose, be it vegan, gluten-free, or any other specialty. Familiarity with dietary restrictions, food preferences, and ingredient alternatives is essential for creating unique and appealing menus. Understanding food safety and hygiene practices is crucial to maintain the highest standards and ensure customer satisfaction. Knowledge of portion control, plating techniques, and food presentation will elevate the overall dining experience for your clients. Additionally, knowing how to handle various types of events, from small gatherings to large weddings, is vital for catering success.

Money Needed: Starting a specialty catering business requires a significant initial investment, primarily in commercial-grade kitchen equipment and utensils. Costs can vary depending on the scale of your operations and the complexity of your menu. Renting or leasing a commercial kitchen space may be necessary if you don't have access to a suitable kitchen. Obtaining necessary licenses and permits to operate a food business legally may also incur expenses. Initial expenses for marketing, branding, and creating a professional website to showcase your services are also important considerations.

Profit Potential: The profit potential in a specialty catering business can be lucrative, particularly if you can successfully target a niche market with high demand. Catering for specialty dietary needs often commands premium pricing, allowing for higher profit margins. As word of mouth and positive reviews spread, you can attract repeat customers and gain new clients through referrals. Building lasting relationships with clients and earning their trust can lead to long-term partnerships for various events and occasions, further increasing your profit potential.

Pros: The opportunity to cater to a specific niche market with a passion for unique cuisine and dietary preferences. Flexibility to create customized menus that cater to various dietary restrictions and preferences. Potential for repeat business and referrals through satisfied clients. Ability to stand out in a competitive catering industry by offering specialized services. The satisfaction of providing delicious and healthy meals that align with clients' values.

Cons: The significant initial investment in kitchen equipment, licenses, and marketing. The challenge of sourcing high-quality specialty ingredients that meet the niche requirements. Potential limitations in the target market size compared to general catering services. The need for continuous research and menu innovation to keep up with evolving dietary trends. The added pressure of meeting specific dietary needs and avoiding cross-contamination for customers with allergies.

Tips: Research your target market thoroughly to understand their preferences and needs. Build a diverse menu with a mix of familiar dishes and unique specialties to cater to various tastes. Source ingredients from reliable suppliers who can provide high-quality, specialty products. Focus on exceptional customer service to build positive relationships with clients. Leverage social media platforms and food-related communities to promote your specialty catering services.

Do's: Do create a professional and user-friendly website to showcase your specialty catering services. Do invest in high-quality ingredients and presentation to deliver outstanding dishes. Do maintain clear communication with clients to understand their dietary needs and preferences. Do provide tasting sessions to potential clients to showcase the quality of your food. Do stay updated on the latest dietary trends and innovations in specialty catering.

Don'ts: Don't compromise on food safety and hygiene practices. Don't overextend your menu to the point of diluting your specialty offerings. Don't neglect marketing efforts; consistent promotion is essential for attracting new clients. Don't overpromise or overcommit; ensure you can deliver what you promise to clients. Don't underestimate the power of positive reviews and customer testimonials in building your reputation.

In conclusion, starting a specialty catering business offers a rewarding opportunity to showcase your culinary expertise while catering to the unique dietary preferences and needs of your target market. By acquiring the necessary knowledge, investing wisely, and delivering exceptional service and cuisine, you can establish a successful specialty catering venture. Embrace the challenges and opportunities that come with catering to a niche market, and with dedication and creativity, you can delight your clients and carve a niche for yourself in the world of specialty catering.

## 43. Providing premium car detailing and protection services

Before delving into the side hustle of providing premium car detailing and protection services, it's essential to comprehend the knowledge required, financial investments, profit potential, as well as the pros and cons associated with this venture. This comprehensive guide will equip you with the necessary information, valuable tips, and do's and don'ts to help you establish a successful and profitable premium car detailing and protection business. Let's explore the details!

Knowledge Needed: To excel in the premium car detailing and protection industry, you need a solid understanding of automotive detailing techniques and products. Familiarity with various car surfaces, such as paint, leather, glass, and metal, is crucial for selecting the appropriate cleaning and protection products. Knowledge of different detailing tools and equipment, including microfiber cloths, polishing machines, and specialized brushes, is essential to achieve professional results. Understanding the intricacies of paint correction and protection techniques will help restore and maintain the pristine appearance of vehicles. Additionally, knowing how to identify and address specific car detailing challenges, such as swirl marks, water spots, and stains, is critical for delivering top-notch services.

Money Needed: Starting a premium car detailing and protection business requires a significant upfront investment in high-quality detailing equipment and products. This includes microfiber towels, polishing compounds, ceramic coatings, wax, sealants, and other detailing chemicals. Purchasing professional-grade polishing machines and steam cleaners is essential for achieving superior results. Moreover, investing in protective gear for yourself, such as gloves and eye protection, is crucial to ensure safety during the detailing process. Additionally, you'll need to allocate funds for marketing and advertising to promote your premium services and reach potential customers.

Profit Potential: The profit potential in the premium car detailing and protection industry can be substantial, especially if you establish a reputation for delivering exceptional results and cater to high-end clientele. Premium car detailing commands premium pricing, allowing for higher profit margins compared to standard detailing services. As you build a loyal customer base through word of mouth and positive reviews, you can expect repeat business and gain new clients through referrals. Offering additional services, such as paint correction and ceramic coatings, can further increase your profit potential, as these services often come with higher price tags.

Pros: Opportunity to cater to luxury car owners and high-end clientele. Higher profit margins due to premium pricing for specialized services. Ability to build a reputation for excellence in the car detailing industry. Potential for repeat business and referrals through satisfied customers. The satisfaction of transforming vehicles into pristine and protected works of art.

Cons: Significant initial investment in high-quality detailing equipment and products. Time-consuming nature of premium car detailing and protection services. The need for attention to detail and precision to achieve professional results. Competitive market with other established car detailing businesses. Dependency on weather conditions, as some detailing tasks may be affected by rain or extreme temperatures.

Tips: Invest in the best quality detailing products and equipment to deliver exceptional results. Focus on building a strong online presence with a professional website and social media platforms. Offer personalized packages and services to cater to specific customer preferences. Provide excellent customer service to create a positive and lasting impression on clients. Showcase before-and-after photos of your work to highlight the quality of your services.

Do's: Do conduct thorough research on the best detailing products and techniques in the industry. Do offer additional services like paint correction and ceramic coatings to increase revenue. Do prioritize customer satisfaction and aim for excellence in every detailing job. Do create a strong brand identity and market your premium services effectively. Do stay updated on the latest trends and advancements in car detailing and protection.

Don'ts: Don't compromise on the quality of detailing products and equipment to cut costs. Don't overlook the importance of safety measures during the detailing process. Don't rush through detailing jobs; take the time to deliver meticulous results. Don't promise services beyond your expertise or capabilities. Don't neglect marketing efforts; consistent promotion is essential for attracting new clients.

In conclusion, providing premium car detailing and protection services offers a lucrative opportunity to cater to high-end customers and showcase your expertise in automotive detailing. With a solid understanding of detailing techniques, a substantial initial investment in equipment and products, and a focus on delivering exceptional results, you can establish a successful and profitable premium car detailing and protection business. Embrace the challenges

and rewards of catering to luxury car owners, and with
dedication and passion for automotive detailing, you can
build a reputable brand that stands out in the competitive car
care industry.

## 44. Investing in dividend stocks or index funds

Before delving into the side hustle of investing in dividend
stocks or index funds, it's crucial to understand the
knowledge required, financial commitment, profit potential,
and the pros and cons associated with this venture. This
comprehensive guide will equip you with the necessary
information, valuable tips, and do's and don'ts to help you
navigate the world of dividend investing and index funds.
Let's explore the details!

Knowledge Needed: Investing in dividend stocks or index
funds requires a fundamental understanding of financial
markets and investment principles. Familiarize yourself with
basic concepts such as risk and return, diversification, and
the power of compounding. Understanding financial
statements and key financial ratios will help you evaluate the
health and profitability of individual companies before
investing in their stocks. Additionally, learning about
different investment strategies and asset allocation will aid
in making informed decisions about your portfolio. Staying
updated on market trends and economic indicators is
essential to adjust your investment strategy as needed.

Money Needed: The amount of money needed to start
investing in dividend stocks or index funds can vary

depending on your investment goals and risk tolerance. For dividend stocks, you can begin with a small amount, as you have the option to reinvest dividends over time and benefit from compounding. On the other hand, investing in index funds may require a larger initial sum to achieve diversification across multiple companies or sectors. Keep in mind that investing is a long-term commitment, and regular contributions or reinvesting dividends will help grow your investment over time.

Profit Potential: Investing in dividend stocks or index funds offers the potential for both capital appreciation and passive income through dividends. Dividend stocks provide a consistent income stream, and if you reinvest dividends, you can benefit from compound growth. Index funds, which track the performance of a specific market index, can offer broad market exposure and potential long-term growth. While stock market fluctuations may impact short-term returns, historical data suggests that investing in the stock market can yield positive returns over the long run.

Pros: Opportunity for long-term wealth creation through capital appreciation and dividend reinvestment. Diversification through index funds reduces individual company risk. Passive income generation through dividends, especially in dividend-focused portfolios. Flexibility to adjust investment strategy based on changing market conditions. Access to the potential growth of successful companies and market sectors.

Cons: Risk of short-term market volatility impacting portfolio value. Dividend cuts or eliminations by companies can affect income flow. The need for research and monitoring of individual stocks or funds in your portfolio. Possible fees and expenses associated with index funds or brokerage accounts. No guaranteed returns, and past performance may not predict future results.

Tips: Start investing early to benefit from the power of compounding over time. Diversify your portfolio to spread risk across different industries and sectors. Consider dividend aristocrats – companies with a history of consistently increasing dividends. Focus on companies with strong fundamentals and a history of stable earnings. Rebalance your portfolio periodically to maintain your desired asset allocation.

Do's: Do research and understand the companies or index funds you plan to invest in. Do set clear investment goals and align your risk tolerance accordingly. Do practice patience and long-term thinking; investing is not a get-rich-quick scheme. Do seek advice from financial experts or consider consulting a financial advisor. Do continue learning and stay informed about market trends and economic developments.

Don'ts: Don't make investment decisions based solely on short-term market fluctuations. Don't put all your money into a single stock or sector, as it increases risk. Don't panic and sell during market downturns; consider the long-term perspective. Don't let emotions drive investment decisions; remain disciplined and rational. Don't invest money you can't afford to lose; always prioritize financial security.

In conclusion, investing in dividend stocks or index funds can be a rewarding side hustle that offers the potential for capital growth and passive income. With a solid understanding of financial markets, a thoughtful investment strategy, and a long-term perspective, you can build a diversified portfolio that aligns with your financial goals and risk tolerance. Keep in mind the importance of continuous learning and staying disciplined in your investment approach, and over time, your side hustle in the world of dividend investing and index funds can pave the way towards financial success and security.

## 45. Starting an online course or coaching business

Before embarking on the side hustle of starting an online course or coaching business, it's essential to understand the knowledge required, financial commitment, profit potential, and the pros and cons associated with this venture. This comprehensive guide will equip you with the necessary information, valuable tips, and do's and don'ts to help you navigate the world of online education and coaching. Let's delve into the details!

Knowledge Needed: Starting an online course or coaching business demands expertise in your chosen subject matter. You must possess in-depth knowledge and a strong understanding of the topic you plan to teach or coach others on. Whether it's a specific skill, industry, or personal development area, your expertise will serve as the foundation for your offerings. Additionally, familiarity with online teaching platforms and instructional design will aid in creating engaging and effective course content. Understanding how to connect with your audience and tailor your teachings to their needs is crucial for success.

Money Needed: The financial investment required to launch an online course or coaching business can vary depending on your chosen platform, marketing strategy, and course development. Creating high-quality content may involve expenses such as video recording equipment, editing software, and graphic design services. Furthermore, marketing efforts to reach your target audience may include advertising costs, website development, and email marketing tools. However, starting an online business often has lower overhead compared to traditional brick-and-mortar ventures.

Profit Potential: The profit potential of an online course or coaching business can be significant, especially as it grows over time. Successful courses with valuable content can attract a large number of students, leading to a steady stream of revenue. Additionally, offering coaching services allows you to charge premium rates for personalized attention and expertise. Once your courses are created, they can become passive income streams, generating revenue even as you focus on other aspects of your business. However, it's crucial to remember that building a profitable online business requires dedication, marketing efforts, and continuous improvement.

Pros: Flexibility to work from anywhere and set your own schedule. The opportunity to share your expertise and knowledge with a global audience. Scalability – the ability to reach a large number of students or clients. Potential for passive income through evergreen courses. Personal satisfaction from helping others achieve their goals and growth.

Cons: Initial time and financial investment in course creation and marketing. Competitive market with a need for unique selling points. The challenge of consistently marketing and promoting your courses. Potential for fluctuations in student enrollments and revenue. Responsibility for handling customer support and inquiries.

Tips: Narrow down your niche and target a specific audience to stand out in the market. Create high-quality content that addresses the pain points and needs of your target audience. Utilize various media formats, such as videos, worksheets, and quizzes, to enhance engagement. Offer free or low-cost content to build trust and attract potential customers. Collect feedback from students or clients to improve and refine your offerings.

Do's: Do thorough market research to identify demand and competition in your chosen niche. Do create a marketing plan to promote your courses or coaching services effectively. Do build an email list to nurture relationships with potential customers. Do stay updated on industry trends and best practices in online education and coaching. Do invest in professional branding and website design to establish credibility.

Don'ts: Don't underestimate the importance of a clear and compelling course description. Don't overprice your courses or coaching services without offering commensurate value. Don't neglect ongoing customer support and engagement with your audience. Don't rush the course creation process; prioritize quality over quantity. Don't be discouraged by initial challenges; building a successful online business takes time and perseverance.

In conclusion, starting an online course or coaching business can be a rewarding side hustle with considerable profit potential. By leveraging your expertise, effectively marketing your offerings, and continuously improving your content, you can attract a loyal audience and generate revenue while helping others achieve their goals. While it requires a significant investment of time and effort upfront, the potential for scalability and passive income makes this side hustle a viable and fulfilling endeavor. Remember to stay committed, stay connected with your audience, and continuously adapt to the evolving landscape of online education and coaching for long-term success.

## 46. Building and flipping websites

Before diving into the side hustle of building and flipping websites, it's essential to understand the necessary knowledge, financial investment, and profit potential associated with this venture. This comprehensive guide will equip you with the information, valuable tips, and do's and don'ts to navigate the world of website flipping successfully. Let's delve into the details!

Knowledge Needed: Building and flipping websites require a solid foundation in web development and design. You should be proficient in programming languages like HTML, CSS, and JavaScript, as well as familiar with content management systems (CMS) like WordPress. Understanding user experience (UX) and search engine optimization (SEO) principles is crucial to create attractive and functional websites that rank well on search engines. Additionally, having basic graphic design skills and an eye for aesthetics can enhance the appeal of your websites to potential buyers.

Money Needed: The financial investment in building and flipping websites can vary significantly, depending on the complexity and scale of your projects. It may involve expenses such as domain registration, website hosting, premium themes, and plugins. If you plan to outsource certain tasks, such as graphic design or content creation, these costs should also be considered. Additionally, investing in advertising and marketing to attract potential buyers can contribute to your overall expenses. While website flipping can be started with a modest budget, having more funds at your disposal can allow you to tackle larger and more profitable projects.

Profit Potential: The profit potential in website flipping can be lucrative, especially if you can identify market trends and create websites with high demand. Successful flips can yield a considerable return on investment, with some websites selling for hundreds or even thousands of dollars. The ability to scale the business by working on multiple projects simultaneously can lead to a steady stream of profits.

However, it's important to note that website flipping is not without risks, and not every project will yield substantial profits. Some flips may require holding onto the website for an extended period before finding the right buyer, affecting your overall profit potential.

Pros: Potential for high returns on successful flips. Flexibility to work from anywhere with an internet connection. Opportunity to showcase your creativity and technical skills. Scalability – the ability to work on multiple projects simultaneously. Possibility of generating passive income through websites with recurring revenue streams.

Cons: Initial time and effort required to build and optimize websites for sale. Fluctuations in the website marketplace and buyer demand. The risk of investing in websites that may not sell or yield significant profits. Competition in the website flipping industry, requiring unique selling points to stand out. The need for ongoing research and adaptation to stay relevant in the market.

Tips: Identify profitable niches or industries with high demand for websites. Optimize websites for search engines to attract potential buyers. Showcase websites with appealing designs and functionality. Provide comprehensive documentation and support materials to enhance the value of your websites. Network and collaborate with other website flippers to gain insights and potential partnerships.

Do's: Do conduct thorough research on market trends and buyer preferences. Do build a portfolio of successful website flips to showcase your expertise. Do invest in a professional and user-friendly website for your flipping business. Do focus on creating websites with evergreen content and revenue streams. Do stay up-to-date with industry trends and technological advancements.

Don'ts: Don't rush into website flips without proper planning and research. Don't overprice your websites; consider market value and demand. Don't neglect website maintenance and security to ensure long-term viability. Don't rely solely on one platform to sell your websites; explore multiple marketplaces. Don't underestimate the importance of responsive and mobile-friendly website design.

In conclusion, building and flipping websites can be a profitable and exciting side hustle for those with the necessary web development skills and an eye for market trends. It offers the potential for significant returns on successful flips and the opportunity to showcase creativity and technical expertise. However, it requires careful planning, ongoing research, and adaptability to navigate the competitive website flipping industry successfully. By understanding the intricacies of website creation, optimization, and marketing, and implementing effective strategies, you can increase your chances of building and flipping websites that yield substantial profits. Remember to stay patient, keep learning, and be open to exploring new opportunities in this dynamic and rewarding side hustle,

## 47. Developing and selling mobile apps

Before embarking on the side hustle of developing and selling mobile apps, it's essential to comprehend the required knowledge, financial investment, and profit potential associated with this venture. This comprehensive guide will equip you with the information, valuable tips, and do's and don'ts to navigate the world of mobile app development and sales successfully. Let's delve into the details!

Knowledge Needed: Developing and selling mobile apps requires a strong foundation in software development and programming. You should be proficient in programming languages like Java or Kotlin for Android app development and Swift for iOS app development. Familiarity with app development frameworks, APIs, and software development kits (SDKs) is essential to create functional and user-friendly apps. Understanding user experience (UX) design principles and mobile app trends is crucial to develop apps that resonate with the target audience. Knowledge of app store guidelines and submission processes for both the Google Play Store and Apple App Store is also necessary.

Money Needed: The financial investment in developing and selling mobile apps can vary significantly, depending on the complexity and scope of your projects. Expenses may include app development tools, software licenses, app store registration fees, and marketing and promotional costs. If you plan to outsource certain aspects of app development, such as graphic design or quality assurance testing, these costs should also be considered. Additionally, ongoing maintenance and updates for the apps can incur recurring expenses. While app development can be started with a modest budget, having more funds at your disposal can allow you to tackle more ambitious projects and invest in effective marketing strategies.

Profit Potential: The profit potential in developing and selling mobile apps can be substantial, especially if you create apps that meet specific market needs and gain popularity. Successful apps can generate revenue through app sales, in-app purchases, and advertisements. The ability to scale your app portfolio and target a global audience can lead to consistent profits. Additionally, if your app gains a loyal user base, you can explore options for subscription-based models or premium features to increase revenue. However, it's important to note that not all apps will achieve significant profitability, and competition in the app marketplace can be fierce, affecting your overall profit potential.

Pros: Potential for substantial profits with successful and popular apps. Flexibility to work remotely and at your own pace. Opportunity to showcase creativity and technical skills. Possibility of recurring revenue through in-app purchases or subscriptions. Ability to target a global audience and reach millions of users.

Cons: Initial time and effort required for app development, testing, and optimization. The risk of investing in apps that may not gain traction or generate significant revenue. Competition in the app market, requiring unique and innovative app ideas to stand out. The need for ongoing updates and maintenance to keep apps relevant and functional. Challenges in marketing and promoting apps to reach a wider audience.

Tips: Identify target market needs and pain points to develop apps with high demand. Optimize app performance and user experience for positive reviews and ratings. Implement effective marketing strategies to promote and gain visibility for your apps. Consider user feedback and reviews to continuously improve and update your apps. Utilize analytics tools to track user engagement and app performance.

Do's: Do conduct thorough market research and competitor analysis before developing your apps. Do prioritize app security and data privacy to build user trust. Do focus on creating apps with intuitive user interfaces and seamless functionality. Do explore monetization options that align with your app's value proposition. Do leverage social media and online communities to connect with potential app users.

Don'ts: Don't rush into app development without a clear plan and target audience in mind. Don't neglect app testing and quality assurance to ensure a smooth user experience. Don't overcomplicate app features; prioritize simplicity and usability. Don't ignore user feedback and reviews; use them to improve your apps. Don't rely solely on organic downloads; invest in marketing and promotion to reach a broader audience.

In conclusion, developing and selling mobile apps can be a rewarding and profitable side hustle for those with a strong background in software development and a keen eye for market trends. It offers the potential for significant returns with successful apps that meet specific market needs and resonate with users. However, it requires careful planning, ongoing updates, and effective marketing strategies to navigate the competitive app marketplace successfully. By staying informed about industry trends, prioritizing user experience, and implementing smart monetization strategies, you can increase your chances of developing and selling mobile apps that achieve substantial profitability. Remember to stay patient, learn from user feedback, and continuously improve your apps to create a sustainable and rewarding side hustle in the exciting world of mobile app development and sales.

## 48. Creating and selling software or plugins

Before diving into the side hustle of creating and selling software or plugins, it's crucial to understand the necessary knowledge, financial investment, and profit potential associated with this venture. This comprehensive guide will equip you with valuable information, tips, and do's and don'ts to navigate the world of software development and sales successfully. Let's explore the details!

Knowledge Needed: Creating and selling software or plugins requires a strong foundation in software development and programming. You should be proficient in programming languages such as Java, C++, Python, or JavaScript, depending on the type of software you want to create. Understanding software design principles, algorithms, and data structures is essential to develop efficient and functional programs. Familiarity with software development tools, integrated development environments (IDEs), and version control systems is also beneficial. Knowledge of the target platform or operating system, whether it's desktop, web, or mobile, is crucial to tailor your software to the intended audience.

Money Needed: The financial investment in creating and selling software or plugins can vary significantly, depending on the complexity and scope of your projects. Expenses may include software development tools, licenses, cloud hosting, and domain registration. If you plan to hire additional developers or designers to assist with the project, these costs should also be considered. Additionally, marketing and promotional expenses, such as website hosting, online advertising, and attending industry events, can contribute to your overall financial investment. While software development can be started with a modest budget, having more funds at your disposal can allow you to tackle larger projects and reach a broader audience.

Profit Potential: The profit potential in creating and selling software or plugins can be substantial, especially if your products meet specific market needs and gain popularity. Successful software can generate revenue through one-time purchases, subscription models, or licensing fees. Additionally, selling plugins for widely-used software platforms can attract a large customer base. As your software gains traction, you can explore opportunities for upselling premium features or offering ongoing support and updates for a fee. However, it's important to recognize that not all software products will achieve significant profitability, and competition in the software market can be fierce, impacting your overall profit potential.

Pros: Potential for significant profits with successful and widely-used software. Flexibility to work remotely and manage your own schedule. Opportunity to showcase creativity and technical skills through innovative software solutions. Possibility of recurring revenue through subscription-based models or ongoing support. Ability to target a global audience and reach millions of potential customers.

Cons: Initial time and effort required for software development, testing, and optimization. The risk of investing in software that may not gain traction or generate significant revenue. Competition in the software market, necessitating unique and valuable software ideas. The need for ongoing updates and customer support to maintain software functionality and relevance. Challenges in marketing and promoting software to reach a wider audience.

Tips: Identify market gaps and pain points to develop software that addresses specific needs. Optimize software performance and user experience to attract positive reviews and recommendations. Implement effective marketing strategies to promote and gain visibility for your software. Offer free trials or demo versions to allow users to experience the value of your software before purchasing. Utilize user feedback to continuously improve and update your software.

Do's: Do conduct thorough market research and competitor analysis before developing your software. Do prioritize software security and data privacy to build user trust. Do focus on creating user-friendly software with intuitive interfaces. Do offer clear documentation and customer support to assist users with any issues. Do establish a pricing strategy that aligns with your software's value and market demand.

Don'ts: Don't rush into software development without a clear plan and target audience in mind. Don't neglect software testing and quality assurance to ensure a seamless user experience. Don't overcomplicate software features; prioritize simplicity and usability. Don't ignore user feedback and suggestions; use them to improve your software. Don't rely solely on organic downloads; invest in marketing and promotion to reach a broader audience.

In conclusion, creating and selling software or plugins can be a rewarding and profitable side hustle for those with a strong background in software development and a keen understanding of market trends. It offers the potential for significant returns with successful products that cater to specific market needs and resonate with users. However, it requires careful planning, ongoing updates, and effective marketing strategies to navigate the competitive software market successfully. By staying informed about industry trends, prioritizing user experience, and implementing smart monetization strategies, you can increase your chances of creating and selling software that achieves substantial profitability. Remember to stay patient, learn from user feedback, and continuously improve your software to establish a sustainable and rewarding side hustle in the exciting world of software development and sales.

## 49. Providing specialized consulting services

Before delving into the side hustle of providing specialized consulting services, it's essential to comprehend the necessary knowledge, financial investment, and profit potential associated with this endeavor. This comprehensive guide will equip you with valuable information, tips, and do's and don'ts to navigate the world of consulting successfully. Let's explore the details!

Knowledge Needed: Providing specialized consulting services demands a deep understanding of the specific field or industry you plan to advise on. You should possess expertise, experience, and a proven track record in the subject matter. Whether it's marketing, finance, human resources, or any other domain, your knowledge should be up-to-date with the latest trends, best practices, and regulations. Excellent communication and interpersonal skills are essential to engage clients, understand their needs, and offer tailored solutions. Additionally, consulting often involves analyzing data, conducting research, and presenting recommendations, so analytical and problem-solving skills are crucial.

Money Needed: The financial investment in providing specialized consulting services can vary depending on the scope and nature of your consulting practice. Initial costs may include setting up a professional website, creating marketing materials, and obtaining any necessary certifications or licenses. Depending on your industry, you may need to invest in software tools or resources to facilitate data analysis and research. Additionally, networking and attending industry events might entail travel and associated expenses. While starting a consulting business can be relatively low-cost compared to other ventures, it's essential to allocate funds for marketing and ongoing professional development.

Profit Potential: The profit potential in specialized consulting services can be substantial, especially when you establish yourself as an expert in your field and build a loyal client base. As a consultant, you can charge premium fees for your specialized knowledge and services, leading to higher revenue per client engagement. Long-term consulting contracts or retainer agreements can provide stable income streams. Additionally, successful consulting often leads to word-of-mouth referrals and testimonials, further expanding your client base and profit potential. However, it's crucial to recognize that building a successful consulting business takes time and effort, and income may vary depending on the number and scope of consulting projects you undertake.

Pros: Opportunity to utilize and share your specialized knowledge and expertise. Flexibility to set your own schedule and work independently. Potential for high earning potential with premium fees for consulting services. Variety of clients and industries to work with, keeping work interesting and diverse. Opportunity to make a significant impact on your clients' businesses or projects.

Cons: Competitive consulting market, requiring differentiation and strong value proposition. Initial challenges in building a client base and establishing credibility. Time-consuming nature of consulting engagements, especially with extensive projects. Balancing client demands and expectations with personal time and work-life balance. The potential for occasional periods of uncertainty between consulting projects.

Tips: Identify your unique value proposition and what sets you apart from other consultants. Develop a clear and compelling consulting service offering with defined deliverables. Network extensively to build relationships with potential clients and industry peers. Seek testimonials and case studies from satisfied clients to showcase your expertise. Leverage digital marketing channels to reach a broader audience and attract clients online.

Do's: Do conduct thorough research to understand your target market and its needs. Do communicate clearly and effectively with clients to manage expectations. Do stay updated on industry trends and best practices to offer cutting-edge solutions. Do provide tangible and measurable results to demonstrate the value of your services. Do establish transparent pricing and terms to avoid misunderstandings with clients.

Don'ts: Don't overcommit or take on projects that fall outside your area of expertise. Don't promise unrealistic outcomes or guarantees to clients. Don't neglect ongoing professional development to stay relevant in your field. Don't undersell your services or undervalue your expertise. Don't ignore feedback from clients; use it to improve and refine your consulting services.

In conclusion, providing specialized consulting services can be a fulfilling and financially rewarding side hustle for those with deep expertise in a particular field. It offers the flexibility to work independently and make a meaningful impact on clients' businesses. By investing in your knowledge and expertise, developing a strong value proposition, and leveraging effective marketing strategies, you can attract clients and build a successful consulting practice. However, it's important to be patient, persistent, and proactive in networking and marketing efforts to establish yourself as a credible and sought-after consultant. Remember to stay updated on industry trends, actively seek client feedback, and continuously enhance your consulting services to thrive in the competitive world of specialized consulting.

## 50. Event planning and coordination services

Before diving into the side hustle of event planning and coordination services, it's crucial to understand the knowledge needed, financial investment required, and profit potential associated with this venture. This comprehensive guide will equip you with valuable information, tips, and do's and don'ts to navigate the world of event planning successfully. Let's explore the details!

Knowledge Needed: Event planning and coordination require a diverse skill set and knowledge in various areas. As an event planner, you should possess excellent organizational and time management skills to manage multiple tasks and deadlines effectively. Communication and negotiation skills are essential for collaborating with clients, vendors, and event attendees. Creativity is crucial for designing unique and memorable events that meet clients' expectations. Additionally, knowledge of event logistics, budgeting, contract management, and risk assessment is necessary to execute successful events. Staying updated on industry trends, technologies, and best practices is vital to provide cutting-edge services.

Money Needed: The financial investment in starting an event planning and coordination business can vary significantly depending on the scale and scope of events you plan to manage. Initial costs may include creating a professional website, marketing materials, and investing in event planning software or tools. Networking and attending industry events may involve travel and associated expenses. Additionally, as you grow your business, you may need to allocate funds for event insurance, event permits, and hiring event staff. While starting small and working on smaller events can be cost-effective, as you take on more significant and complex events, your financial investment may increase.

Profit Potential: The profit potential in event planning and coordination services can be substantial, especially as you build a reputation for delivering successful events. Event planners typically charge a percentage of the event budget or a flat fee for their services. As you take on larger and more prestigious events, your earning potential increases. Moreover, building long-term relationships with clients can lead to recurring business and referrals, further expanding your profit potential. However, it's essential to recognize that the event planning industry can be competitive, and profitability may vary depending on the number and scale of events you manage.

Pros: Opportunity to showcase creativity and design unique events. Flexibility to work independently and manage your own schedule. Possibility of high earning potential, especially with large-scale events. Opportunity to build strong relationships with clients and vendors. The satisfaction of seeing successful events come to life.

Cons: Competitive event planning market, requiring differentiation and exceptional service. Time-consuming nature of event planning, especially with large-scale events. The pressure of managing multiple tasks and deadlines simultaneously. The need to handle unexpected challenges and last-minute changes during events. Balancing personal time and work-life when managing events on weekends and holidays.

Tips: Define your niche and target market to specialize in specific types of events. Build a professional portfolio showcasing your past event successes. Cultivate strong relationships with vendors and suppliers to secure the best deals. Offer exceptional customer service to exceed clients' expectations. Embrace technology to streamline event planning processes and communications.

Do's: Do communicate clearly and effectively with clients and vendors. Do stay updated on industry trends and best practices. Do create detailed event timelines and budgets to stay organized. Do prioritize client satisfaction and responsiveness. Do prepare for unforeseen circumstances with contingency plans.

Don'ts: Don't overcommit or take on events beyond your capacity. Don't overlook contracts and legal agreements; ensure clarity on responsibilities. Don't underestimate the importance of attention to detail in event planning. Don't ignore feedback from clients and attendees; use it to improve your services. Don't overlook the value of networking and building industry connections.

In conclusion, event planning and coordination services can be a rewarding and profitable side hustle for those with strong organizational and creative skills. The potential to design memorable events, build lasting client relationships, and earn a respectable income makes this side hustle an attractive option. By investing in your knowledge, showcasing past successes, and offering exceptional customer service, you can stand out in the competitive event planning market. However, it's essential to be prepared for the time-consuming nature of event planning and the challenges that may arise during event execution. With careful planning, attention to detail, and a focus on exceeding client expectations, you can thrive in the exciting world of event planning and coordination.

# 51. Real estate investing (e.g., rental properties)

Before delving into the world of real estate investing, it's crucial to understand the knowledge needed, financial requirements, and profit potential associated with this side hustle. Real estate investing, particularly rental properties, offers the potential for passive income and long-term wealth building. However, it also comes with risks and responsibilities. This comprehensive guide will provide you with valuable insights, tips, and do's and don'ts to embark on a successful real estate investment journey.

Knowledge Needed: Real estate investing requires a solid understanding of the local housing market and economic conditions. Knowledge of property types, neighborhoods, and rental demand will help you make informed investment decisions. Familiarity with real estate laws, rental regulations, and tax implications is essential for legal and financial compliance. Additionally, you should have basic financial literacy to evaluate potential deals, calculate returns, and manage finances effectively. Understanding property management and maintenance is crucial for providing quality living spaces to tenants and ensuring property longevity. Continuous learning and staying updated on industry trends will help you navigate the ever-changing real estate landscape.

Money Needed: The financial investment in real estate investing can vary widely based on location, property type, and your investment strategy. Some investors start with smaller properties or partner with others to pool resources. Down payments for rental properties typically range from

15% to 25% of the property's purchase price. Additionally, you should allocate funds for property inspections, closing costs, and potential renovations or repairs. Besides the initial investment, you should have sufficient reserves to cover vacancies, unexpected repairs, and ongoing property management expenses. As you expand your real estate portfolio, access to financing and maintaining a good credit score become crucial for securing favorable loan terms.

Profit Potential: Real estate investing offers multiple avenues for profit, primarily through rental income and property appreciation. Rental income provides a steady cash flow, and if managed well, it can cover mortgage payments and generate passive income. Over time, property values may appreciate, allowing you to build equity and potentially sell the property at a profit. Additionally, leveraging other people's money (mortgages) to acquire properties allows you to benefit from property appreciation and rental income without tying up all your own funds. However, it's essential to consider potential risks, such as market fluctuations, vacancies, and unexpected expenses, which can impact profit potential.

Pros: Potential for long-term wealth building through property appreciation. Steady rental income generating passive cash flow. Diversification of investment portfolio with tangible assets. Tax advantages, including deductions for mortgage interest and property expenses. Control over property decisions and improvements.

Cons: Risk of property market fluctuations affecting property values. Time and effort required for property management and tenant relations. Potential vacancies leading to temporary loss of rental income. Financial risks, including mortgage defaults and unexpected expenses. Legal and regulatory compliance obligations.

Tips: Research and understand the local real estate market and rental demand. Calculate potential returns and cash flow accurately before purchasing a property. Start with a conservative investment approach to mitigate risks. Build a team of professionals, including real estate agents, property managers, and contractors. Invest in well-maintained properties that align with your investment strategy.

Do's: Do conduct thorough due diligence on properties and their potential for rental income. Do set aside reserves for vacancies and unexpected repairs. Do maintain open communication with tenants and address maintenance promptly. Do network and build relationships with other real estate investors. Do educate yourself continuously on real estate investing best practices.

Don'ts: Don't overlook the importance of property inspections before purchasing. Don't overextend your finances; ensure you can cover mortgage payments and expenses. Don't neglect property maintenance, as it can impact property value and tenant satisfaction. Don't rush into investment decisions without careful evaluation. Don't ignore local laws and regulations regarding rental properties.

In conclusion, real estate investing, particularly rental properties, can be a lucrative side hustle with the potential for long-term wealth creation. By acquiring the necessary knowledge, conducting thorough research, and making informed investment decisions, you can build a successful real estate portfolio. However, it's essential to be prepared for the responsibilities of property management, market fluctuations, and financial risks. By implementing sound investment strategies, maintaining open communication with tenants, and continuously educating yourself, you can navigate the real estate investment landscape successfully and potentially achieve financial independence through your side hustle.

## 52. Trading cryptocurrencies or forex

Before delving into the world of cryptocurrency and forex trading, it's crucial to understand the knowledge needed, financial requirements, and profit potential associated with this side hustle. Cryptocurrency and forex trading offer the potential for high returns but also come with significant risks. This comprehensive guide will provide you with valuable insights, tips, and do's and don'ts to embark on a successful trading journey.

Knowledge Needed: Trading cryptocurrencies or forex requires a solid understanding of financial markets, technical analysis, and trading strategies. You should be familiar with the fundamentals of blockchain technology and how cryptocurrencies function. In forex trading, knowledge of macroeconomic factors, geopolitical events, and interest rate decisions is essential. Technical analysis involves studying price charts and indicators to identify potential market trends and entry/exit points. Risk management and emotional discipline are crucial for successful trading. Continuous learning and staying updated on market trends and news will help you make informed trading decisions.

Money Needed: The financial investment in cryptocurrency and forex trading can vary widely based on your trading strategy and risk tolerance. Both markets allow traders to start with relatively small amounts of capital, but it's essential to only trade with money you can afford to lose. In cryptocurrency trading, you'll need funds to open an account on a cryptocurrency exchange. In forex trading, you'll need to deposit money with a forex broker. You should also allocate funds for potential losses, as trading involves inherent risks. Some traders opt for leverage to magnify potential returns, but it also increases the risk of significant losses.

Profit Potential: Cryptocurrency and forex trading offer the potential for high returns due to the volatility of these markets. Successful traders can profit from price fluctuations and market trends. Some traders have achieved significant wealth through trading. However, it's essential to understand that trading involves substantial risks, and there is no guarantee of profits. It's possible to lose a significant portion or all of your investment. Profit potential depends on your trading strategy, risk management, and market conditions.

Pros: Potential for high returns and wealth accumulation. Access to 24/7 markets for cryptocurrency trading. Diversification opportunities with different cryptocurrencies or forex pairs. The ability to start with relatively small amounts of capital. Opportunities to use leverage to increase trading position sizes.

Cons: High volatility and risk of significant losses. The lack of regulation in the cryptocurrency market can lead to scams and fraud. Emotional challenges, as trading can be psychologically demanding. The need for continuous learning and staying updated on market trends. The potential for market manipulation and sudden price movements.

Tips: Educate yourself thoroughly about trading concepts and strategies. Start with a demo account to practice trading without risking real money. Develop a trading plan with clear entry and exit strategies and risk management rules. Avoid making impulsive decisions based on emotions or FOMO (fear of missing out). Use stop-loss orders to limit potential losses. Start with a small trading size and gradually increase as you gain experience and confidence.

Do's: Do research and analyze the assets you're trading thoroughly. Do use risk management techniques, such as setting stop-loss orders. Do keep a trading journal to track your performance and learn from your trades. Do stay disciplined and stick to your trading plan. Do diversify your portfolio to manage risk.

Don'ts: Don't invest money you cannot afford to lose. Don't chase after quick profits without a solid strategy. Don't trade based on rumors or unverified information. Don't let emotions drive your trading decisions. Don't over-leverage your trades, as it increases the risk of significant losses.

In conclusion, cryptocurrency and forex trading can offer significant profit potential, but they come with high risks and require a solid understanding of market dynamics and trading strategies. By educating yourself, developing a trading plan, and using risk management techniques, you can navigate these markets more effectively. However, it's essential to remember that trading involves inherent risks, and losses are possible. As with any investment, it's crucial to start small, gain experience, and continuously improve your trading skills. Only trade with money you can afford to lose, and be prepared for the emotional challenges that come with trading. With discipline, patience, and continuous learning, you can increase your chances of success in the world of cryptocurrency and forex trading.

## 53. FOREX Leverage

It's crucial to emphasize that trading forex involves a high level of risk, including the possibility of losing more money than originally invested. This is due to the concept of leverage, which is commonly offered by forex brokers to magnify potential profits. However, it also amplifies potential losses.

When trading with leverage, you only need to put up a fraction of the total trade size as a deposit, known as the margin. The rest of the trade value is effectively borrowed from the broker. While this can significantly increase your trading position and potential returns, it also means that even small price movements can lead to significant losses.

For example, if you have a leverage of 1:100 and invest $1,000, your total trading position would be $100,000 (100 times your initial investment). A price movement of just 1% against your trade could result in a $1,000 loss, wiping out your entire investment.

Furthermore, forex markets are highly liquid and can experience rapid and unpredictable price fluctuations, especially during major economic events or geopolitical developments. As a result, traders need to be prepared for the possibility of substantial losses, even if they initially intended to risk only a small portion of their capital.

To mitigate the risk of losing more than invested, traders must exercise strict risk management practices. Setting stop-loss orders is essential, as it automatically closes the trade if the market moves against your position beyond a predetermined level. Traders should also avoid over-leveraging their trades and should only risk a small percentage of their capital on any single trade.

Overall, trading forex offers potential profit opportunities, but it is essential to approach it with caution and be fully aware of the risks involved. Beginners should start with a demo account to practice their strategies and gain experience without risking real money. Additionally, continuous learning and staying updated on market conditions are critical to becoming a successful forex trader.

## 54. Buying and selling domain names

Before delving into the world of buying and selling domain names, it's essential to understand the knowledge required, the money needed to get started, and the profit potential. "Domain flipping," as it's often called, involves purchasing domain names with the intent to sell them later at a higher price.

To start this side hustle, you need to develop knowledge in several key areas. First, you must learn how to conduct domain market research to identify valuable domain names with potential resale value. Understanding domain valuation is crucial, as you'll need to evaluate domain names based on factors like keyword relevance, brandability, length, and demand.

Staying up-to-date with industry trends is vital, as market demand for domain names can shift rapidly. You should be aware of popular keywords and emerging industries that may drive the demand for specific domain names. Additionally, familiarize yourself with trademark and copyright laws to avoid infringing on others' intellectual property rights.

Negotiation skills are essential in this venture, as you'll need to effectively negotiate with potential buyers and sellers to maximize your profits. It's crucial to know how to persuade buyers to pay the desired price for your domain names while getting the best deals when purchasing domains.

In terms of finances, you'll need enough capital for the initial investment in purchasing domain names. The cost can vary significantly, from a few dollars to hundreds or even thousands, depending on the perceived value of the domain. Keep in mind that domain registration fees are recurring, as domains typically need renewal annually. If you plan to hold domains for an extended period, consider budgeting for hosting and maintenance costs.

The profit potential in domain flipping can be lucrative. Successful flips can yield substantial returns, with some domain names selling for millions of dollars. Additionally, if you invest in premium domain names and generate revenue through advertising or leasing, you can enjoy passive income streams. As businesses increasingly establish an online presence, the demand for attractive domain names continues to grow, creating ample opportunities for profitable sales.

However, like any venture, domain flipping comes with its pros and cons. One advantage is the flexibility it offers; you can work from anywhere with an internet connection, providing convenience and autonomy. Moreover, the low entry barrier makes it accessible to people with limited funds, allowing them to enter the market without substantial capital.

On the other hand, the domain market can be unpredictable, with varying demand for different names. It may take time to find buyers willing to pay the desired price, leading to potential holding costs. Moreover, not all purchased domain names will appreciate in value, and some may even become worthless over time, leading to potential losses.

To succeed in domain flipping, it's crucial to conduct thorough research to identify valuable domain names and potential buyers. Starting with low-cost domain names can help gain experience and reduce risks. Building a diverse portfolio of domain names can increase your chances of finding interested buyers.

Networking with domain investors and industry experts can provide valuable insights and potentially lead to finding buyers. Patience is essential; wait for the right time to sell your domain names for the best possible price. Keep records of your domain acquisitions, sales, and expenses for accounting purposes, and don't let valuable domains expire; ensure timely renewals to retain ownership.

To avoid pitfalls, do not register domain names that may infringe on existing trademarks or copyrights. Additionally, avoid overestimating a domain's value and paying exorbitant prices; stick to reasonable valuations. Rushing into buying domains without thorough research can lead to poor investment decisions.

In summary, domain flipping can be a profitable side hustle with the right knowledge, strategy, and patience. By understanding market trends, conducting thorough research, and adopting smart negotiation tactics, you can enter this industry with confidence and potentially turn it into a lucrative venture. However, remember that success may not be immediate, and domain flipping requires a combination of skill, intuition, and a keen eye for identifying valuable domain names.

## 55. Offering financial planning or investment advice

Before venturing into the side hustle of offering financial planning or investment advice, it's crucial to understand the knowledge required, the money needed to start, and the profit potential. Providing financial guidance to individuals or businesses requires expertise in various areas, including personal finance, investment strategies, tax planning, and retirement planning.

To start this side hustle, you'll need a strong foundation in financial concepts, such as budgeting, saving, and debt management. Knowledge of different investment vehicles, like stocks, bonds, mutual funds, and real estate, is essential. Familiarity with tax laws and regulations is crucial to help clients optimize their tax situations and maximize returns. Additionally, staying informed about market trends, economic conditions, and global events can aid in providing timely and relevant advice.

Obtaining relevant certifications or licenses is often necessary to offer financial planning or investment advice professionally. Common certifications include Certified Financial Planner (CFP), Chartered Financial Analyst (CFA), and Registered Investment Advisor (RIA). These designations indicate a high level of expertise and professionalism, instilling trust and confidence in potential clients.

The money needed to start this side hustle can vary significantly. If you already have the required certifications and experience, the startup costs may primarily involve setting up a home office, purchasing necessary software or tools, and marketing your services. However, if you need to obtain certifications or licenses, there will be additional costs associated with exam fees, study materials, and continuing education.

The profit potential in offering financial planning or investment advice can be substantial. As your client base grows, you can charge fees for your services, either as a percentage of the assets you manage or through hourly rates or flat fees. Building a strong reputation and delivering positive results can lead to referrals and a steady stream of clients, further increasing your earnings.

One advantage of this side hustle is the potential for recurring income. Clients often seek ongoing advice and support, providing a stable source of revenue. Additionally, you can offer specialized services, such as retirement planning or estate planning, which may command higher fees due to their complexity and long-term value.

However, there are also some challenges and cons to consider. Providing financial advice comes with significant responsibility, as the advice you give can have a direct impact on your clients' financial well-being. It's essential to act ethically, prioritize your clients' best interests, and maintain transparency in your recommendations.

Competition in the financial advisory industry can be fierce, especially in larger markets. To stand out, you'll need to differentiate yourself through your expertise, personalized approach, and exceptional customer service. Building trust with clients takes time and effort, so be prepared to invest in building strong relationships.

When starting, consider offering free or discounted consultations to attract clients and showcase your expertise. This can help build your client base and establish your reputation as a reliable financial advisor. Encourage satisfied clients to provide testimonials and reviews, as positive word-of-mouth can be invaluable in growing your business.

In providing financial planning or investment advice, it's crucial to remain unbiased and avoid any conflicts of interest. Disclose any potential conflicts, such as receiving commissions from certain products, to maintain transparency and trust with your clients.

Continuing education is essential in this field to stay up-to-date with changes in financial regulations, tax laws, and investment trends. Attend industry conferences, webinars, and workshops to expand your knowledge and expertise.

Finally, consider the importance of communication skills. Being able to explain complex financial concepts in simple terms and tailoring your advice to each client's individual needs is crucial in providing valuable and effective guidance.

In conclusion, offering financial planning or investment advice can be a rewarding and profitable side hustle. With the right knowledge, certifications, and dedication to ethical practices, you can help clients achieve their financial goals while building a successful and reputable business. Remember to stay informed, continuously improve your skills, and prioritize your clients' best interests to thrive in this competitive industry.

## 56. Running a subscription box service

Before starting a side hustle like running a subscription box service, it's essential to understand the knowledge required, the money needed to start, and the profit potential. A subscription box service involves curating and delivering themed packages of products to customers on a regular basis, typically monthly. This business model requires a combination of creativity, marketing skills, logistics management, and customer service expertise.

To begin this side hustle, you should have a good understanding of your target market and their preferences. Researching and identifying niche markets with high demand for subscription boxes will be crucial in ensuring the success of your venture. Knowledge of product sourcing, pricing, and inventory management will also be essential to curate boxes that offer value to subscribers while maintaining profitability.

Having a creative eye for product curation and package design will help you create attractive and unique subscription boxes that stand out in the market. Understanding customer preferences and trends in your niche will allow you to continually offer fresh and exciting products in each box.

Marketing skills are vital for promoting your subscription box service and attracting subscribers. Knowledge of digital marketing, social media, and email marketing will be valuable in reaching your target audience and building brand awareness. Additionally, understanding customer acquisition and retention strategies will play a significant role in the long-term success of your subscription box service.

To manage the logistics of running a subscription box service, you'll need to have strong organizational and time management skills. Coordinating with suppliers, managing inventory, and ensuring timely and accurate shipments to customers will be critical to maintain customer satisfaction.

The money needed to start a subscription box service can vary depending on the scale and complexity of your business. You'll need to budget for product sourcing and inventory, packaging materials, shipping costs, and marketing expenses. Building a website or e-commerce platform to showcase your subscription box offerings and handle subscriptions will also require financial investment.

The profit potential in running a subscription box service can be substantial if you can attract a steady stream of subscribers. With a successful business model, economies of scale can come into play, allowing you to negotiate better deals with suppliers and reduce costs. As your subscriber base grows, you can generate recurring revenue, providing a stable income stream.

One advantage of this side hustle is the opportunity to foster a strong sense of community among your subscribers. By curating boxes around shared interests or values, you can create a loyal customer base that feels connected to your brand. Engaging with subscribers through social media, newsletters, and special promotions can enhance this sense of community and encourage long-term loyalty.

However, there are also some challenges and cons to consider. Competition in the subscription box market can be intense, especially in popular niches. It's essential to find a unique selling proposition that differentiates your service from others and appeals to your target audience.

Careful financial planning is necessary to ensure that your subscription box service remains profitable. The costs of product sourcing, packaging, and shipping can add up quickly, so it's crucial to balance these expenses with the subscription fees you charge.

Customer churn is another challenge in the subscription box industry. To retain subscribers, focus on delivering consistent value and exciting products in each box. Responding promptly to customer inquiries and addressing any issues or concerns will also contribute to positive customer experiences.

To start your subscription box service, consider offering different subscription plans, such as monthly, quarterly, or annual options. Providing flexibility in subscription lengths can attract customers with varying preferences and budgets.

Investing in high-quality packaging and branding will enhance the unboxing experience for subscribers. The presentation of your subscription box can leave a lasting impression and encourage word-of-mouth referrals.

Offering customization options, where subscribers can personalize their boxes to some extent, can increase customer satisfaction and retention. Gathering feedback from subscribers and incorporating their suggestions into future boxes can also strengthen your relationship with customers.

When marketing your subscription box service, focus on creating engaging and shareable content that highlights the value and uniqueness of your offerings. Collaborating with influencers or partnering with complementary brands can also expand your reach and attract new subscribers.

In conclusion, running a subscription box service can be a rewarding and profitable side hustle with the right knowledge, planning, and execution. Understanding your target market, managing logistics efficiently, and providing excellent customer experiences are essential elements for success. Stay attentive to trends, continually refresh your offerings, and prioritize customer satisfaction to thrive in this dynamic and competitive industry.

## 57. Starting a food truck or catering business

Starting a food truck or catering business can be an exciting and rewarding side hustle, but it also requires careful planning and consideration. To succeed in this venture, you'll need to have a thorough understanding of the food industry, including local regulations, health and safety standards, and permits required to operate a mobile food business in your area. Familiarize yourself with the target market and local food trends to tailor your menu accordingly.

Having culinary skills and a passion for food can give your business a competitive edge. While formal culinary training is not always necessary, being able to create delicious and unique dishes will be advantageous. Experiment with different recipes and conduct taste tests to develop a menu that stands out. Consider catering to different dietary preferences, such as vegan or gluten-free options, to widen your customer base.

Creating a comprehensive business plan is essential. Your plan should outline your concept, target market, menu, pricing strategy, and marketing approach. Define your startup costs, operating expenses, and projected revenue. Research potential locations for your food truck or catering service, taking into account foot traffic, local events, and competitor presence.

The startup costs for a food truck or catering business can vary significantly depending on factors such as the size and condition of the food truck, equipment, initial inventory, branding, and marketing expenses. Generally, the initial investment can range from $50,000 to $200,000 or more. It's essential to have enough capital to cover startup costs and sustain the business until it becomes profitable.

The profit potential in the food truck or catering business can be promising, but it will depend on factors such as your menu, pricing, location, and marketing efforts. Successful food trucks can generate annual revenues ranging from $50,000 to $250,000 or more. Catering businesses, especially those that cater to large events or corporate clients, can potentially earn higher revenues. However, keep in mind that the profit margin can vary, and it may take time to establish a loyal customer base and achieve steady profits.

Choosing the right location for your food truck is crucial to attract customers. Research high-traffic areas, such as business districts, parks, and event venues, and secure the necessary permits and licenses to operate in those areas. Some cities have strict regulations on where food trucks can operate, so compliance with local laws is essential.

Craft a diverse and appealing menu that offers a balance of classic favorites and unique specialties. Consider seasonal ingredients and be open to making adjustments based on customer feedback. Pricing your items competitively while maintaining a reasonable profit margin is crucial. Take into account food costs, overhead expenses, and competitor pricing when setting your menu prices.

Develop a strong brand identity and logo that reflects your concept and resonates with your target audience. Utilize social media platforms, food truck directories, and local events to market your business. Engage with your audience through interactive content and promotions. Positive online reviews and word-of-mouth referrals can significantly impact the success of your food truck or catering business.

Consistency in food quality, taste, and presentation is essential for building a loyal customer base. Train your staff (if applicable) to uphold high standards and prioritize excellent customer service. Address customer feedback and resolve issues promptly to maintain a positive reputation.

Efficient logistics and operations are vital for the smooth running of your food truck or catering business. Plan your daily routes and schedules for food truck operations to maximize exposure to potential customers. For catering, ensure timely delivery and set up for events. Invest in equipment maintenance and ensure compliance with health and safety regulations to avoid interruptions to your business.

Pros of Starting a Food Truck or Catering Business:

- Mobility: Food trucks offer the flexibility to reach different customer segments by changing locations based on demand and events.
- Low Overhead: Compared to brick-and-mortar restaurants, food trucks typically have lower operating costs.
- Unique Selling Point: Food trucks can create a sense of novelty and excitement, attracting customers looking for a unique dining experience.
- Catering Opportunities: In addition to regular food truck operations, catering for events, weddings, and corporate functions can be lucrative.
- Direct Customer Interaction: Food truck owners have the opportunity to interact directly with customers, gaining valuable feedback and building relationships.

- Creative Expression: The food truck or catering business allows for creative expression through menu creation and presentation.

Cons of Starting a Food Truck or Catering Business:

- Seasonal Challenges: Depending on the location, food truck businesses may face seasonal fluctuations in demand.
- Weather Dependency: Inclement weather can impact foot traffic and food truck operations.
- Space Limitations: The limited kitchen space in food trucks may restrict the variety of items on the menu.
- Competition: The food industry is competitive, with numerous food trucks and caterers vying for customers' attention.
- Maintenance Costs: Regular maintenance of the food truck and equipment can add to operating expenses.
- Health and Safety Regulations: Compliance with health and safety regulations can be complex and time-consuming.

Tips for Success:

- Be Authentic: Offer a unique and authentic culinary experience that sets you apart from competitors.
- Build Relationships: Network with other food vendors, event organizers, and potential clients to create business opportunities.
- Monitor Expenses: Keep a close eye on your financials, and be prepared to make adjustments if expenses exceed projections.

- Adaptability: Stay adaptable to changing market trends and customer preferences.
- Focus on Quality: Consistently deliver high-quality food and excellent customer service.
- Social Media Presence: Utilize social media platforms to showcase your offerings and engage with customers.

Dos and Don'ts:

- Do Conduct Market Research: Understand your target market and competition before launching your food truck or catering service.
- Do Create a Memorable Brand: Invest in branding and a visually appealing food truck design to attract customers.
- Do Prioritize Customer Experience: Focus on providing exceptional customer service to build loyalty and positive reviews.
- Don't Neglect Marketing: Allocate a budget for marketing and promotion to reach a broader audience.
- Don't Overextend Yourself: Start with a manageable menu and gradually expand based on customer demand and feedback.
- Don't Compromise on Quality: Consistently deliver high-quality dishes to ensure customer satisfaction and repeat business.

In conclusion, starting a food truck or catering business can be a fulfilling and profitable side hustle with the right knowledge, planning, and dedication. Understanding the industry, conducting thorough market research, and creating a unique culinary experience will be key to success. Stay adaptable to market trends, provide excellent customer service, and adhere to health and safety regulations to build a loyal customer base and achieve long-term profitability.

## 58. Launching a podcast with sponsorships and ads

Starting a podcast with sponsorships and ads can be an exciting and potentially lucrative side hustle. However, it requires careful planning, dedication, and knowledge of the podcasting industry. Before starting your podcast, consider the following key factors.

To start a podcast with sponsorships and ads, you'll need to acquire various skills and knowledge. Familiarize yourself with the fundamentals of podcasting, such as recording, editing, and publishing episodes. Understanding how to use recording equipment and editing software is crucial to producing high-quality content. Develop a clear niche and content strategy for your podcast, ensuring it resonates with your target audience. Consistent, valuable, and engaging content is essential to attract and retain listeners.

Learn basic audio editing skills to enhance the quality of your episodes and provide a polished listening experience. Good editing can make a significant difference in the overall perception of your podcast. Understand the process of hosting your podcast on a reliable platform and distributing it to major podcast directories like Apple Podcasts and

Spotify. Choose a hosting provider that fits your needs and budget.

Learn how to effectively market and promote your podcast to attract a loyal audience. Utilize social media, email marketing, collaborations with other podcasters, and guest appearances to increase your reach. Research how podcast sponsorships and ad sales work and how to approach potential advertisers. Understand the different types of sponsorships and negotiate fair deals. Familiarize yourself with podcast analytics tools to track your audience's demographics and listening habits. This data can help you tailor your content and attract more advertisers.

Starting a podcast with sponsorships and ads will involve some upfront costs and ongoing expenses. Invest in quality recording equipment, such as microphones, headphones, and recording software. While it's essential to have good audio quality, you don't need to break the bank. There are various budget-friendly options available. Choose a reputable podcast hosting platform that offers the storage and bandwidth necessary for your episodes. Hosting costs can vary based on the size of your podcast and the provider you choose.

Allocate a budget for marketing efforts, such as social media ads, promotions, and collaborations. Building an audience takes time and effort, and investing in targeted advertising can help speed up the process. Consider hiring professional services for cover art design, website development, or transcription services, depending on your needs and expertise.

The profit potential of a podcast with sponsorships and ads varies depending on factors such as audience size, niche, and advertiser interest. As your podcast gains traction and attracts a sizable audience, you can approach relevant sponsors for advertisements. Sponsored segments or mentions can generate revenue based on a CPM (cost per thousand impressions) model or a flat rate.

Consider partnering with companies whose products or services align with your podcast's theme. You can earn a commission for every sale generated through your unique affiliate link. Offer exclusive or bonus content to your loyal listeners through a paid subscription model. Patreon or other membership platforms can facilitate this revenue stream.

You can run crowdfunding campaigns on platforms like Kickstarter or Indiegogo to finance special projects or improve the production quality of your podcast. As your podcast grows in popularity, you can host live events or workshops, selling tickets for entry and merchandise at these gatherings.

Pros of Starting a Podcast with Sponsorships and Ads:

Flexibility: Podcasting allows you to create content on topics you're passionate about and work on your schedule.

Audience Connection: Podcasting enables you to build a loyal and engaged audience, fostering a sense of community.

Income Diversification: With multiple revenue streams, you're not solely reliant on one source of income.

Brand Building: A successful podcast can establish you as an authority or thought leader in your niche.

Creative Expression: Podcasting offers a creative outlet to share your ideas and connect with like-minded individuals.

Cons of Starting a Podcast with Sponsorships and Ads:

Time-Intensive: Podcasting requires significant time and effort, from content planning to promotion.

Initial Investment: There are upfront costs for equipment, hosting, and marketing.

Competition: The podcasting landscape is competitive, and standing out may take time.

Revenue Uncertainty: Income from sponsorships and ads may fluctuate, especially in the early stages.

Technical Challenges: Dealing with audio editing and equipment troubleshooting can be challenging for beginners.

Tips for Success:

Define Your Niche: Identify a specific target audience and focus on providing valuable content for them.

Consistency is Key: Stick to a regular podcasting schedule to keep your audience engaged.

Engage with Your Audience: Encourage listener feedback, answer questions, and consider featuring listener submissions.

Networking: Collaborate with other podcasters or influencers in your niche to cross-promote and expand your reach.

Optimize for Discoverability: Use relevant keywords and tags to improve your podcast's visibility on podcast directories.

Do's:

Be authentic and passionate about your content. Authenticity resonates with audiences.

Plan your episodes and script where necessary. This helps maintain focus and coherence.

Invest in good audio quality. Listeners appreciate clear and pleasant-sounding content.

Engage with your audience on social media and through emails to build a community.

Research and approach sponsors and advertisers who align with your values and audience.

Don'ts:

Overspend on equipment when starting. Start with essential equipment and upgrade as you grow.

Neglect marketing and promotion. Even the best content needs visibility to attract listeners.

Ignore feedback from your audience. Listen to their needs and preferences.

Rely solely on sponsorships for income. Diversify revenue streams for stability.

Be discouraged by slow growth in the beginning. Building an audience takes time and effort.

In conclusion, starting a podcast with sponsorships and ads can be a fulfilling and potentially profitable side hustle. To succeed, invest in knowledge and equipment, plan your content carefully, engage with your audience, and explore various revenue streams. While it may take time to see significant profit, the sense of community and creative satisfaction make podcasting a rewarding venture.

## 59. Importing and selling products from overseas

Starting a side hustle of importing and selling products from overseas requires a comprehensive understanding of the process, necessary knowledge, financial requirements, and the potential for profits. It involves various steps and considerations that can significantly impact the success of the venture.

To succeed in this side hustle, you need to understand import regulations, customs duties, tariffs, and taxes of both your country and the exporting country. This knowledge is crucial for smooth customs clearance and compliance with legal requirements. Market research is essential to identify profitable products with demand in your target market. Analyze competitors, consumer preferences, and potential pricing strategies to make informed decisions.

Verifying the authenticity and reliability of overseas suppliers is vital. Evaluate product quality, certifications, and manufacturing processes to ensure you provide high-quality products to your customers. Logistics and shipping knowledge is essential to efficiently manage the movement of products from the source to your destination. You need to learn about shipping methods, lead times, and freight forwarding.

Understanding international currency exchange rates and choosing secure payment methods is critical to avoid financial risks. Being aware of cultural norms and business practices in the exporting country is essential for building strong relationships with suppliers and navigating potential communication challenges. Developing negotiation skills is crucial to secure favorable terms and pricing with suppliers.

You should also be familiar with the necessary paperwork and contracts involved in international trade, such as purchase agreements, shipping contracts, and insurance documents.

Importing products from overseas often requires a significant initial investment to purchase inventory, cover shipping costs, and handle customs fees. Shipping and logistics expenses can add up, especially if you're dealing with large or bulky products. Importing products may involve paying customs duties and taxes, which can vary depending on the product and country of origin.

You need to budget for marketing and promotional efforts to create brand awareness and attract customers to your products.

Importing products from overseas can be more cost-effective, allowing you to sell at competitive prices and potentially increase profit margins. Accessing products not readily available in your local market can attract customers seeking unique and niche items, increasing the potential for profit. It can help you tap into international markets, expanding your customer base and profit potential.

Offering high-quality imported products can enhance your brand reputation and attract loyal customers willing to pay a premium. With successful operations, importing and selling products from overseas can be scaled up to increase profitability.

However, there are cons to consider. Dealing with shipping, customs, and international suppliers can present logistical challenges and delays. Exchange rate fluctuations can impact costs and profit margins. Ensuring consistent product quality may be challenging when dealing with overseas suppliers. Language barriers and different time zones can complicate communication with suppliers. Adhering to import regulations and compliance requirements can be complex and time-consuming.

Tips:

Start small with a limited product selection and gradually expand as you gain experience and understanding of the market. Build strong relationships with reliable suppliers to ensure a steady supply of quality products. Test the market with a smaller batch of products before committing to large quantities to gauge demand.

Factor in shipping times when planning inventory levels to avoid stockouts. Utilize e-commerce platforms and social media to reach a broader audience and attract customers globally.

Do's:

Thoroughly research potential suppliers, their reputation, and the quality of their products. Calculate all costs involved, including shipping, customs, and taxes, to determine pricing and profit margins accurately.

Prioritize customer service and respond promptly to inquiries and concerns. Invest in marketing efforts to create brand awareness and attract customers. Stay updated on import regulations and compliance requirements to avoid legal issues.

Don'ts:

Rush into large orders without testing the market and assessing product demand. Overlook cultural differences and etiquette when dealing with overseas suppliers.

Compromise on product quality to cut costs; prioritize delivering value to your customers. Ignore customer feedback; use it to improve your product offerings and services.

Rely on a single supplier; have backup options to mitigate potential risks.

In conclusion, launching a side hustle of importing and selling products from overseas can be rewarding with the right knowledge and approach. Conduct thorough research, plan meticulously, and establish strong supplier relationships to ensure a successful venture. While there are challenges and risks, the potential for profit and market expansion can make it a lucrative and exciting business opportunity. With careful execution and adherence to best practices, you can build a thriving business that caters to diverse customer needs and preferences.

## 60. Providing home renovation or remodeling services

Starting a side hustle in home renovation or remodeling services can be a lucrative and fulfilling venture. However, before diving in, it's crucial to have the necessary knowledge, financial planning, and awareness of the potential profit and challenges involved in this industry.

To succeed in this venture, you must have a solid foundation in home construction, renovation techniques, and building codes. Additionally, having a good eye for design and the ability to create functional and aesthetically pleasing spaces is vital for customer satisfaction. Proficiency in project management is also essential to ensure timely completion of renovations, efficient use of resources, and effective communication with clients and subcontractors.

Familiarity with local building codes, zoning regulations, and permit processes is crucial to avoid legal issues and delays in projects. Furthermore, adhering to safety regulations is critical to protect both workers and clients during the renovation process.

Having knowledge of marketing strategies and excellent customer service skills are necessary to attract clients and build a strong reputation in the industry. As for the financial aspect, a significant investment is required to purchase or rent the necessary tools and equipment for home renovations, such as power tools, ladders, and safety gear.

Moreover, liability insurance and workers' compensation insurance are essential to protect against potential accidents and liabilities. A reliable vehicle for transporting tools and materials is necessary for a home renovation business. Budgeting for marketing and advertising expenses is vital to reach potential clients and grow the business.

Estimating material costs accurately is crucial to pricing projects competitively and ensuring profitability. Additionally, having a financial buffer for unexpected expenses or slow periods is essential to sustain the business during challenging times.

The profit potential in the home renovation and remodeling industry can be significant, especially for skilled and reputable contractors. With proper pricing, efficient project management, and a steady flow of clients, a home renovation business can yield substantial profits. Positive word-of-mouth referrals from satisfied clients can also lead to a steady stream of projects.

Pros:

One of the primary advantages of starting a home renovation side hustle is the fulfilling nature of the work. For those passionate about transforming spaces and creating dream homes for clients, home renovation can be deeply rewarding.

Additionally, there is a high demand for renovation services as homeowners often seek to update and improve their properties, ensuring a steady demand for skilled contractors. The diversity of home renovation projects also offers opportunities to work on various projects and expand skills.

As a side hustle, home renovation allows for flexible scheduling and the potential to scale the business gradually. A successful side hustle can evolve into a full-time business with increased profitability and market recognition.

Cons:

The home renovation industry can experience seasonal fluctuations, affecting the flow of projects and income. Managing multiple projects simultaneously may require effective time management skills as home renovations can be time-consuming and physically demanding, involving heavy lifting and long hours.

The market can be competitive, requiring contractors to differentiate themselves through quality work and exceptional service. Managing client expectations and potential project changes can also be challenging and may require strong communication skills.

Tips:

When starting a home renovation side hustle, it is advisable to begin with smaller projects to gain experience and build a portfolio. Accurately estimating project costs and setting competitive pricing is essential to attract clients while ensuring profitability.

Focusing on delivering high-quality work is crucial to earning positive reviews and referrals. Building relationships with real estate agents, architects, and other industry professionals can help expand your client base. It is essential to use written contracts that clearly outline project details, timelines, and payment terms to avoid misunderstandings.

Do's:

Maintain open communication with clients throughout the project to address concerns and provide updates. Fulfill project commitments on time and within budget to build trust and credibility.

Continuously improve by staying updated on industry trends, new materials, and construction techniques to deliver innovative solutions. Ensure all required permits and licenses are obtained before commencing any work.

Don'ts:

Avoid taking on more projects than can be efficiently managed to maintain quality and meet deadlines. Prioritize safety measures to protect both workers and clients. Act on client feedback to improve services and client satisfaction. Quality work may suffer if projects are rushed, so prioritize thoroughness and attention to detail.

Starting a home renovation side hustle requires dedication, expertise, and careful planning. By providing quality workmanship, adhering to timelines, and cultivating positive client relationships, you can build a successful and rewarding business in the home renovation industry.

## 61. Providing interior design services

Starting a side hustle in interior design services can be a fulfilling and financially rewarding venture for individuals with a passion for creativity and transforming spaces. However, before embarking on this journey, it is essential to acquire the necessary knowledge, consider the financial implications, and understand the profit potential, along with the pros and cons associated with this field.

Knowledge Needed:

Interior design is a multifaceted field that involves creating aesthetically pleasing and functional spaces for clients. A strong foundation in design principles, color theory, and spatial planning is vital for an interior designer. Understanding different design styles and trends can help cater to diverse client preferences.

Additionally, proficiency in using design software like AutoCAD, SketchUp, and Adobe Creative Suite is crucial for creating detailed design plans and visualizations. Knowledge of building codes and regulations ensures that design plans comply with safety and legal requirements.

Good communication and listening skills are essential to understand clients' needs and translate their vision into tangible design concepts. Strong project management abilities help keep projects on track and within budget.

Money Needed:

Starting an interior design side hustle requires a certain level of financial investment. You may need to invest in design software, a computer, and other essential office supplies. Building a portfolio and marketing your services might involve costs for professional photography, printing, and website development.

While working as a freelancer, you may also need to budget for transportation expenses to visit clients and potential networking events. As your business grows, you might consider investing in a workspace or a design studio to meet with clients and showcase your work.

Profit Potential:

The profit potential in interior design services can be significant, especially for talented and experienced designers. Interior designers often charge clients a combination of fixed fees, hourly rates, or a percentage of the project cost. By setting competitive pricing and managing projects efficiently, interior designers can generate substantial income.

Building a strong reputation and gaining positive client testimonials can lead to increased referrals and more projects. Moreover, specializing in niche markets or targeting high-end clientele can lead to higher fees and profits.

Pros:

Interior design offers a creative and rewarding outlet for designers to express their artistic vision while enhancing living and working spaces for clients. The industry's diversity allows designers to work on various projects, from residential to commercial spaces, which keeps the work interesting and engaging.

Flexibility is another advantage of pursuing interior design as a side hustle, as it allows designers to manage their schedules and balance other commitments. Moreover, the satisfaction of seeing a project come to life and witnessing clients' appreciation can be highly gratifying.

Cons:

Interior design can be a competitive industry, requiring designers to continuously stay updated on design trends and invest in professional development. Securing clients and building a steady stream of projects might take time and effort, especially in the early stages.

Clients may have varying expectations, and managing their preferences and budget constraints can be challenging. Interior designers need to be adaptable and capable of handling multiple projects concurrently, which may be demanding during peak seasons.

Tips:

Build a Strong Portfolio: Compiling your best design projects into a professional portfolio showcases your capabilities and impresses potential clients.

Networking: Attend design events, trade shows, and join professional associations to network with industry peers, potential clients, and collaborators.

Referrals and Testimonials: Request testimonials from satisfied clients and encourage them to refer your services to others as word-of-mouth marketing is powerful in the design industry.

Clear Communication: Ensure you have clear and open communication with clients to understand their preferences, budget, and project requirements.

Branding and Marketing: Develop a strong brand identity and online presence through a professional website, social media, and marketing materials to attract clients.

Do's:

Establish Clear Agreements: Set clear expectations with clients through written contracts that outline the scope of work, fees, timelines, and responsibilities.

Stay Updated: Continuously educate yourself about new design trends, materials, and technologies to offer innovative solutions to clients.

Create Mood Boards: Use mood boards or design presentations to visually communicate design concepts effectively to clients.

216

Prioritize Space Planning: Emphasize functional space planning to ensure the design meets the needs and lifestyle of the client.

Don'ts:

Overpromise and Underdeliver: Avoid committing to unrealistic timelines or budgets that could compromise the quality of the design.

Neglecting Budget Constraints: Always be mindful of your client's budget and avoid proposing design elements that exceed it significantly.

Ignoring Feedback: Listen to client feedback and be open to making necessary revisions to meet their expectations.

Neglecting Building Codes: Ensure that your design complies with local building codes and regulations to avoid legal issues.

Starting a side hustle in interior design can be a gratifying journey for creative individuals with a passion for transforming spaces. By investing in knowledge, refining your skills, and providing exceptional customer service, you can build a successful and thriving interior design business.

## 62. Developing and selling software as a service (SaaS)

Before diving into the world of developing and selling Software as a Service (SaaS), it's essential to understand what SaaS actually means. SaaS is a software distribution model where applications are hosted and maintained by a third-party provider and made available to customers over the internet. As a side hustle, creating and selling SaaS products can be an exciting and potentially profitable venture, but it requires careful planning, technical knowledge, and a solid understanding of the market.

Knowledge Needed:

Technical Expertise: To create SaaS products, you'll need a strong foundation in software development, including programming languages like Python, Java, or Ruby, and knowledge of cloud computing, databases, and API integration. Understanding the principles of software architecture and design patterns is also crucial.

Market Research: Conducting thorough market research is essential to identify potential customers, understand their pain points, and validate your product idea. You should analyze competitors' offerings, pricing strategies, and customer feedback to identify gaps and opportunities in the market.

User Experience (UX) Design: Creating a user-friendly interface and optimizing the overall user experience is essential to attract and retain customers. Understanding UX design principles, conducting usability testing, and gathering user feedback will help you refine and improve your product.

Security: SaaS products handle sensitive user data, so knowledge of cybersecurity and data protection is vital to ensure your product is secure and compliant with regulations. Implementing encryption, access controls, and regular security audits will help protect your customers' data.

Customer Support: Providing excellent customer support is essential for customer satisfaction and product success. You'll need to set up channels for customer inquiries, feedback, and issue resolution, and ensure timely and helpful responses.

Money Needed:

Initial Development Costs: Building a SaaS product requires a significant initial investment in development resources. You may need to hire software developers, UX designers, and possibly a project manager to oversee the process.

Infrastructure and Hosting: SaaS products rely on robust and scalable infrastructure. You'll need to invest in cloud hosting services like AWS, Google Cloud, or Azure to ensure your application can handle increased user demand.

Marketing and Promotion: To attract customers, you'll need to invest in marketing and promotional activities. This may include digital marketing, content creation, social media advertising, and attending industry events.

Ongoing Maintenance and Updates: SaaS products require regular maintenance, bug fixes, and updates. You'll need to budget for ongoing development and support to keep your product running smoothly.

Profit Potential:

The profit potential of a SaaS side hustle can be significant, but it depends on various factors such as the demand for your product, the size of your target market, pricing strategy, and operational costs. Here are some potential sources of revenue for a SaaS business:

Subscription Fees: Most SaaS products operate on a subscription-based model, where customers pay a monthly or annual fee to access the software. The recurring revenue from subscriptions can provide a steady income stream.

Tiered Pricing: Offering different subscription tiers with varying features and levels of service allows you to cater to a broader range of customers and potentially increase revenue.

Add-Ons and Upsells: You can offer additional features or add-on services that customers can purchase to enhance their experience, generating additional revenue.

Free Trials and Freemium Models: Providing free trials or a freemium version of your product can attract more users and potentially convert them into paying customers over time.

Partner and Affiliate Programs: Collaborating with other businesses or running an affiliate program can help expand your reach and bring in additional revenue through referrals.

Pros:

One advantage of starting a SaaS side hustle is its scalability, as these products can efficiently accommodate a growing user base without major infrastructure changes. The subscription-based model provides a steady and predictable income stream, offering stability and ease of financial planning. With an internet-based distribution model, SaaS products can reach customers worldwide, eliminating geographical barriers. Additionally, SaaS products offer flexibility, as they can be accessed from any device with an internet connection, providing convenience and versatility for users.

Cons:

While SaaS side hustles have their merits, they also come with challenges. The initial investment in developing and launching a SaaS product can be substantial, making it difficult for those with limited funds to enter the market. Furthermore, the SaaS industry is highly competitive, making it challenging to stand out among established players. Acquiring and retaining customers is another hurdle, especially in saturated markets where customer loyalty can be hard to maintain. Additionally, building and maintaining a robust and secure SaaS product requires technical expertise and ongoing effort.

Tips:

To increase the chances of success in the SaaS market, aspiring entrepreneurs should validate their product ideas through thorough market research and potential customer feedback. Starting small with a Minimum Viable Product (MVP) can help test the market and gather essential feedback for improvement. Prioritizing user experience is crucial, as a positive UX can lead to customer satisfaction and retention. Investing in marketing strategies is also important for reaching and attracting the target audience effectively. Finally, providing excellent customer support can be a key differentiator for a SaaS business, ensuring prompt responses and helpful solutions.

Do's:

Entrepreneurs entering the SaaS market should conduct comprehensive research and understand their target market's needs before developing their products. Prioritizing security and data protection is essential to gain customer trust and comply with relevant regulations. Continuously monitoring and analyzing user feedback allows for continuous improvement and the addition of necessary features. Investing in reliable and scalable cloud hosting services ensures that the SaaS product can handle increased user demand.

Don'ts:

Rushing the development process is a common mistake that should be avoided. Instead, it is crucial to take the time needed to build a robust and user-friendly SaaS product. Neglecting the importance of customer support can have adverse effects, as unhappy customers may leave negative reviews and harm the business's reputation. Ignoring the competition is another pitfall to avoid; analyzing competitors' strengths and weaknesses can help find ways to differentiate the product. Lastly, neglecting marketing and promotion efforts can hinder the ability to attract customers and drive growth.

Starting a SaaS side hustle can be a rewarding venture with the potential for significant profit and growth. However, it requires careful planning, technical expertise, and a customer-centric approach. By validating your product idea, focusing on user experience, and investing in marketing and customer support, you can increase your chances of success in the competitive SaaS market. Remember that building a successful SaaS business takes time and effort, so stay persistent and continuously adapt based on user feedback and market trends.

## 63. Providing high-end wedding planning services

Starting a side hustle in providing high-end wedding planning services can be a rewarding venture with the potential for substantial profits. However, it also comes with its set of challenges and requirements for success. To ensure a smooth and prosperous journey, aspiring wedding planners should equip themselves with the necessary knowledge, skills, and resources.

First and foremost, a comprehensive understanding of the wedding industry is crucial. As a high-end wedding planner, you must stay updated with the latest trends, popular themes, and cultural traditions. This knowledge will enable you to offer personalized and tailored services to your clients, creating unforgettable experiences that reflect their unique preferences and tastes.

Strong event management skills are also essential for success in this field. As a wedding planner, you will be responsible for overseeing every aspect of the event, from coordinating with vendors to managing the timeline and handling any last-minute challenges that may arise. Effective communication, organizational prowess, and the ability to remain calm under pressure are all key traits of a successful wedding planner.

Building a network of reliable and skilled vendors is vital to provide top-notch services to your clients. Collaborating with experienced florists, photographers, caterers, and other professionals will ensure that your clients' wedding day is executed flawlessly. These partnerships not only elevate the quality of your services but also enable you to negotiate better deals for your clients, enhancing your value proposition.

Creativity is a valuable asset in the wedding planning industry. Clients often seek unique and innovative ideas to make their weddings stand out. Being able to think outside the box and offer creative solutions will set you apart from the competition and win over clients looking for something extraordinary.

As with any business, having a strong understanding of financial management is crucial. You need to establish clear pricing structures, taking into account your time, effort, and overhead costs. Additionally, having a budgeting system in place will help you allocate resources effectively, ensuring profitability while providing exceptional services.

Money needed to start a high-end wedding planning side hustle can vary depending on your location, scope of services, and business model. Initially, you may need to invest in marketing materials, a website, professional photography, and networking events. While you can start small and gradually expand your offerings, setting aside sufficient funds for marketing and initial expenses will set you up for success.

Profit potential in the wedding planning industry can be lucrative, especially in the high-end segment. Clients are often willing to pay a premium for top-tier services and unforgettable experiences. As your reputation grows, and word-of-mouth referrals increase, you can attract more high-paying clients, leading to significant profit margins.

Starting a side hustle in providing high-end wedding planning services comes with its set of advantages. One of the most appealing aspects is the high earning potential that comes with being able to command premium fees. Additionally, being a wedding planner allows for a creative outlet, enabling you to showcase your innovative ideas and design unique and extraordinary weddings. The job can also be incredibly rewarding, as you have the opportunity to help couples create their dream weddings and witness their joy on their special day. Building a strong network of vendors and industry professionals opens doors to potential collaborations and referrals, which can further boost your success. Furthermore, wedding planning offers flexible working hours, making it suitable for those with other commitments.

However, there are also cons to consider when starting a wedding planning side hustle. One of the main challenges is the time-intensive nature of the job. As the event date approaches, the demands can be overwhelming, requiring long hours of preparation and execution. The wedding industry is also known for its seasonal nature, with peak times and lulls throughout the year, which can impact your workload and income. Dealing with the emotions of clients and managing potential conflicts can be challenging and emotionally taxing, making strong emotional intelligence essential. Additionally, the industry is competitive, requiring consistent effort to stand out and attract clients among other talented wedding planners.

To ensure success in the wedding planning industry, there are several essential tips to follow. Building a strong portfolio showcasing past weddings you have planned will demonstrate your skills and expertise to potential clients. Networking is crucial - attending wedding expos, industry events, and joining professional associations will help you expand your network and gain exposure. Providing exceptional customer service is paramount - going above and beyond to exceed client expectations and build strong relationships will lead to positive referrals and recommendations. Embracing technology can streamline processes and enhance efficiency in your planning. Staying organized and keeping detailed records are essential to ensure smooth execution of events.

When offering wedding planning services, it's vital to understand your clients' preferences and vision for their wedding. Listen carefully to their needs and tailor your services accordingly. Open and clear communication with clients and vendors is key to avoiding misunderstandings. Offering personalized services that go beyond cookie-cutter solutions will impress your clients and set you apart from the competition. However, it's crucial not to overcommit and take on more clients than you can handle effectively. Be realistic about your workload to maintain the quality of your services and ensure client satisfaction. Additionally, always have clear and detailed contracts in place to protect both yourself and your clients throughout the planning process.

By considering the pros and cons, following the essential tips, and being mindful of the do's and don'ts, you can establish a successful side hustle in high-end wedding planning. Your ability to provide exceptional services and create unforgettable experiences will contribute to your success in this competitive but rewarding industry.

## 64. Offering home energy efficiency consulting

Starting a side hustle in offering home energy efficiency consulting can be a rewarding venture that not only helps homeowners save on their energy bills but also contributes to environmental sustainability. To embark on this path, you'll need a solid understanding of energy efficiency principles and practices, knowledge of different home systems and appliances, and familiarity with energy-efficient technologies and products. Gaining certifications or accreditations in energy efficiency will add credibility to your services.

In terms of money needed, the initial investment for this side hustle may be relatively low. You'll need to cover the costs of marketing materials, creating a professional website, and possibly obtaining certifications. Additionally, having access to tools and equipment for conducting energy audits, such as infrared cameras and energy monitors, may require some financial investment. However, compared to other businesses, the overhead costs can be manageable, especially if you choose to operate from a home office.

The profit potential in home energy efficiency consulting can be significant, as more homeowners are becoming conscious of their energy consumption and seeking ways to reduce their environmental impact. Your earnings will primarily come from charging for your consulting services. You can structure your fees based on an hourly rate or a flat fee for specific services, such as conducting energy audits and providing detailed recommendations for improvements. Additionally, you may have the opportunity to earn commissions or referral fees by partnering with energy-efficient product vendors and contractors.

Starting a side hustle in offering home energy efficiency consulting has its share of advantages and challenges. On the positive side, there is a high demand for such services as more homeowners are becoming aware of the importance of energy efficiency and sustainability. This growing awareness creates a favorable market for energy consultants to provide their expertise and guidance.

Another advantage is the potential environmental impact. By promoting energy-efficient practices, you'll be contributing to reducing greenhouse gas emissions and promoting environmental conservation. This aspect can be personally fulfilling, knowing that your work is making a positive difference in the world.

The flexibility of operating a home-based business is yet another pro. As an energy consultant, you have the freedom to set your own schedule and choose the projects you take on. This allows for a better work-life balance and the opportunity to pursue other interests alongside your consulting work.

Additionally, the clientele for energy efficiency consulting is diverse. Your potential clients range from individual homeowners looking to improve energy efficiency in their residences to businesses seeking to reduce their operating costs. This diversity offers various opportunities to grow and expand your consulting services.

Despite the promising advantages, there are some challenges to consider. One of the cons is the seasonal fluctuations in demand. The need for energy efficiency consulting may vary depending on the season and economic conditions, which can impact the consistency of projects and income.

Another challenge is the initial marketing effort required to attract clients. As a new energy consultant, you'll need to invest time and resources in marketing and networking to establish your reputation and attract a steady flow of clients.

Technical knowledge is also crucial for this side hustle. To provide valuable and relevant recommendations, you'll need to stay updated on the latest energy-efficient technologies, building systems, and home energy assessments. Keeping up with advancements in the industry can be time-consuming but is essential for maintaining your expertise.

Furthermore, the energy efficiency consulting industry can be competitive. With other consultants and service providers vying for clients, you'll need to differentiate yourself and demonstrate your expertise to stand out in the market.

Lastly, the success of your consulting services is performance-based. The effectiveness of your recommendations may be subject to various external factors, and your clients' satisfaction will be directly linked to the results achieved through the implementation of your advice.

Tips:

Acquire Expertise: Invest in education and training to become knowledgeable about energy-efficient technologies, building systems, and home energy assessments.

Obtain Certifications: Consider obtaining relevant certifications, such as Building Performance Institute (BPI) or Leadership in Energy and Environmental Design (LEED).

Network and Collaborate: Build relationships with contractors, vendors, and organizations in the energy efficiency industry to expand your network and gain referrals.

Market Your Services: Create a professional website, develop informative content, and leverage social media platforms to showcase your expertise and attract clients.

Conduct Comprehensive Audits: When performing energy audits, thoroughly assess a home's energy usage to provide accurate and personalized recommendations.

Do's:

Listen to Clients: Understand their energy-saving goals, comfort concerns, and budget constraints to tailor your recommendations accordingly.

Focus on Energy Payback: Prioritize energy-saving measures that offer reasonable payback periods for your clients.

Offer Practical Solutions: Provide achievable recommendations that homeowners can implement without significant disruptions.

Educate Clients: Explain the benefits of energy-efficient practices and technologies to empower homeowners in making informed decisions.

Stay Updated: Continuously research and stay informed about advancements in energy-efficient technologies and programs.

Don'ts:

Overpromise Results: Be realistic about the potential savings and benefits of energy efficiency upgrades.

Ignore Local Regulations: Familiarize yourself with local building codes and regulations related to energy efficiency to ensure compliance.

Push Unnecessary Upgrades: Avoid recommending unnecessary or expensive upgrades that don't align with your clients' needs and budget.

Disregard Safety: Prioritize safety when conducting energy audits, especially when dealing with gas or electrical systems.

Neglect Follow-ups: Maintain communication with clients after providing recommendations to address any questions or concerns they may have.

In conclusion, offering home energy efficiency consulting can be a lucrative and meaningful side hustle. By acquiring the necessary knowledge, promoting your services effectively, and providing valuable recommendations, you can make a positive impact on homeowners' lives and the environment while building a successful consulting business.

## 65. Starting a custom printing and merchandise business

Starting a side hustle in the custom printing and merchandise business can be an exciting and potentially profitable venture. However, before diving into this field, there are several key factors to consider to ensure your success.

Knowledge needed: To start a custom printing and merchandise business, you'll need a good understanding of the printing process and different printing techniques. Knowledge of graphic design software is essential for creating custom designs for your merchandise. Familiarity with various printing materials and their properties is also crucial for producing high-quality products.

Additionally, understanding market trends and customer preferences is vital for creating appealing and marketable designs. Knowledge of e-commerce platforms and online marketing strategies will be necessary for reaching a broader audience and driving sales.

Money needed: The startup costs for a custom printing and merchandise business can vary depending on the scale and complexity of your operation. You'll need to invest in printing equipment, such as a printer, heat press, or screen printing machine, which can range from a few hundred to several thousand dollars.

Purchasing blank merchandise, such as t-shirts, mugs, or phone cases, to print on will also require upfront capital. Furthermore, investing in graphic design software and other design tools may be necessary.

Additionally, consider the costs of setting up a website or online store to showcase and sell your merchandise. Marketing and advertising expenses will also play a role in attracting customers to your business.

Profit potential: The profit potential in the custom printing and merchandise business can be significant, especially if you can offer unique and high-quality products that appeal to a specific target market. The markup on custom merchandise can be substantial, allowing you to generate a healthy profit margin on each sale.

As your business grows and you gain a loyal customer base, the profit potential will increase. Expanding your product range or offering bulk orders to businesses and organizations can further boost your revenue.

Starting a custom printing and merchandise business can be a rewarding venture, but like any business, it comes with its own set of pros and cons. One of the significant advantages of this side hustle is the opportunity for creative expression. As a custom printing business owner, you can unleash your creativity and bring unique designs to life, which can be fulfilling and enjoyable.

Another pro is the flexibility that comes with running this type of business. You have the freedom to work from home or a small workspace, and you can set your own working hours, allowing you to maintain a work-life balance that suits your needs.

The custom printing and merchandise industry also offers a diverse customer base. Your products can appeal to a broad audience, from individuals looking for personalized gifts to businesses seeking branded promotional items. This diversity can provide multiple revenue streams and opportunities for growth.

Moreover, the overhead costs of starting a custom printing business can be relatively low, especially if you begin small and gradually expand. Compared to other businesses that may require significant initial investment, this can be an attractive aspect for aspiring entrepreneurs.

On the flip side, there are some cons to consider. One of the primary challenges is the high level of competition in the custom printing and merchandise industry. With many online and offline businesses offering similar products, it can be challenging to stand out and attract customers.

Maintaining consistent quality in your prints and merchandise is crucial for customer satisfaction, but it can be difficult, especially when dealing with large order volumes. Ensuring that your designs do not infringe on copyrighted material is another concern to avoid legal complications.

To maximize your chances of success, here are some essential tips to consider. First, focus on niche markets. Finding a specific target audience or niche for your custom merchandise can help you differentiate yourself from the competition and attract a more dedicated customer base.

Prioritize quality in your products and invest in high-quality printing equipment and merchandise. Delivering products that exceed customer expectations will lead to positive reviews and word-of-mouth referrals, boosting your reputation.

Building a strong online presence is crucial in today's digital age. Create a professional website or online store to showcase your designs and make it easy for customers to browse and purchase your products.

Offering excellent customer service is vital for any business, and the custom printing industry is no exception. Respond to customer inquiries promptly, address their concerns, and strive to provide a positive buying experience to encourage repeat business.

When starting your custom printing business, do thorough research. Understand market trends, customer preferences, and your competition to inform your business decisions. This knowledge will help you tailor your offerings to meet the needs and desires of your target audience.

Creating original designs is essential to set yourself apart from competitors. Develop unique and appealing designs that resonate with your target audience and create a recognizable brand identity.

Test your prints on different materials before offering new products to ensure quality and durability. This step is crucial in maintaining the consistency and excellence of your merchandise.

Establish clear policies for shipping, returns, and customer service to avoid misunderstandings and potential conflicts. Having transparent policies will help build trust with your customers.

Networking and collaboration can be beneficial in growing your business. Build connections within the industry and consider collaborating with influencers or other businesses to expand your reach and attract new customers.

While there are many things you should do to succeed in the custom printing and merchandise industry, there are also some important don'ts to keep in mind.

First, don't compromise on quality. Delivering subpar prints or merchandise can damage your reputation and hurt your business in the long run. Always prioritize the quality of your products to ensure customer satisfaction and loyalty.

Avoid violating copyright laws. Use only images and designs that you have the right to use, and always seek permission if needed. This will protect you from potential legal issues and maintain your business's integrity.

When starting your business, avoid overspending on equipment. Begin with essential equipment and gradually invest in upgrades as your business grows and demands increase.

Lastly, don't neglect marketing efforts. Consistent and strategic marketing is essential to attract and retain customers. Utilize social media, influencer collaborations, and targeted advertising to reach your desired customer base.

In conclusion, starting a custom printing and merchandise business can be a fulfilling and profitable side hustle. With the right knowledge, dedication, and creativity, you can build a successful venture that brings joy to your customers and generates revenue for your business. By focusing on quality, customer service, and marketing, you can differentiate yourself in a competitive market and create a thriving custom printing business. Remember to stay informed about industry trends and continuously improve your offerings to meet the ever-changing demands of your customers.

## 66. Offering resume or audition tape review services

Before starting a side hustle offering resume or audition tape review services, there are several important aspects to consider. This type of side hustle can be rewarding, especially if you have expertise in resume writing or reviewing audition tapes. However, it also requires specific knowledge, skills, and understanding of the job market or entertainment industry.

Firstly, having a strong background in resume writing or recruitment is crucial for offering resume review services. You should be familiar with current resume formats, industry-specific keywords, and the best practices for tailoring resumes to different job positions. Additionally, knowledge of various industries and job roles will help you provide valuable insights and suggestions to your clients.

If you're considering offering audition tape review services, experience in the entertainment industry or performing arts can be advantageous. Familiarity with the specific requirements of different auditions, such as theater, film, or music, will enable you to give relevant feedback to aspiring artists or performers.

To start this side hustle, you will need to invest time in creating a professional website or online platform to showcase your services and attract potential clients. You may also need to set up an appointment booking system or establish a communication channel where clients can submit their resumes or audition tapes for review.

Regarding money needed, the initial investment will primarily depend on the cost of creating and maintaining your website or platform. Additionally, you may need to allocate some budget for marketing and advertising to reach your target audience effectively.

Profit potential in resume or audition tape review services can vary. Initially, it may take some time to build a client base and gain credibility in the industry. However, once you establish a reputation for providing high-quality reviews and valuable insights, you can potentially charge higher fees for your services. Repeat business and word-of-mouth referrals can also contribute significantly to your profit potential.

Starting a side hustle offering resume or audition tape review services can be a rewarding venture. The pros of this side hustle include the opportunity to utilize your expertise in recruitment or the entertainment industry to help others succeed in their job search or audition process. The flexibility it offers allows you to choose the number of clients you take on and set your own working hours. Additionally, the remote nature of this work makes it suitable for individuals who prefer to work from home. Providing valuable feedback and improving resumes or audition tapes can have a significant impact on your clients' careers, making it a fulfilling experience. Moreover, working with diverse clients from various industries or artistic backgrounds adds excitement to your work.

However, there are cons to consider as well. Resume or audition tape review is subjective, and different hiring managers or casting directors may have varied preferences.

Some clients may have strong emotional attachments to their resumes or audition tapes, making it challenging to deliver constructive criticism. Attracting clients and building a reputation may require considerable marketing efforts and time investment. Additionally, competition from other professionals offering similar services can be a hurdle.

To succeed in this side hustle, consider these tips and do's. Stay updated on current resume trends, job market demands, and industry-specific requirements. Offer personalized feedback tailored to each individual client, addressing their unique strengths and areas for improvement. Showcase positive testimonials from satisfied clients on your website to build credibility. Network with professionals in your industry or entertainment circles to expand your client base. Develop a marketing strategy, including social media, online advertising, or collaborations with career coaches or talent agencies, to reach your target audience. Maintain a high level of professionalism in all interactions with clients to build trust and credibility.

On the other hand, there are some things you should avoid (don'ts) when offering resume or audition tape review services. Don't overpromise or make exaggerated claims about job placement or audition success. Stay impartial in your feedback and avoid favoring specific industries or artistic styles in your reviews.

Starting a side hustle offering resume or audition tape review services can be a fulfilling and potentially profitable venture. Leveraging your expertise and providing personalized feedback can make a significant impact on clients' career journeys. While it may require effort to establish your business and attract clients, dedication, professionalism, and marketing strategies will contribute to your success. Remember to continuously improve your knowledge and stay updated with industry trends to offer the best possible service to your clients.

"Genius is 1% inspiration, and 99% perspiration."

Thomas A. Edison

www.ingramcontent.com/pod-product-compliance
Lightning Source LLC
Chambersburg PA
CBHW070000300526
45794CB00001B/123